COBOL for Micros

COBOL for Micros

Norman Stang

Newnes Technical Books

Newnes Technical Books
is an imprint of the Butterworth Group
which has principal offices in
London, Boston, Durban, Singapore, Sydney, Toronto, Wellington

First published 1983

© **Butterworth & Co (Publishers) Ltd, 1983**
 Borough Green, Sevenoaks, Kent TN15 8PH, England

British Library Cataloguing in Publication Data

Stang, Norman
 COBOL, for micros
 1 COBOL (Computer program language)
 2 Microprocessors
 I Title
 001 64'24   QA76 73 C25

ISBN 0–408–01342–7

Library of Congress Cataloging in Publication Data

Stang, Norman.
 COBOL for micros.
 Includes index.
 1. COBOL (Computer program language)
 2. Microcomputers—Programming. I. Title.
 II. Title: C.O.B.O.L. for micros.
 QA76.73.C25S73   1983   001.64'24   83–7775

ISBN 0–408–01342–7

Typeset by Phoenix Photosetting, Chatham, Kent
Printed in England by A. Wheaton & Co. Ltd., Exeter

Preface

After leaving university in the mid 1960s I learnt to program in assembly languages and later in COBOL and BASIC. In those relatively early days the notion of using a standardised business computer programming language appealed to me, and COBOL, though by no means perfect, fitted the bill extremely well. My support for the language has not waned even with the introduction over the year of new wonder languages such as PL-1, Pascal and the like.

These newer languages, and specialist languages designed for the layman user of database systems, were thought by many to lead to the demise of COBOL. And the growing use of microcomputers in business was forecast to be yet another nail in COBOL's coffin. However, recent developments have shown that any obituary notices for COBOL were essentially premature. Indeed its life has been prolonged by the success of interactive versions specially produced for microcomputers. CIS COBOL is only one such version among several currently available. Whether it is the best version is not for me to say, but it is certainly popular among business microcomputer users and software houses.

My experience with CIS COBOL has made it abundantly clear to me that COBOL programming requirements for a microcomputer are different from those associated with a mainframe computer. On the whole, the object code is efficient in terms of memory storage requirements and processing of data is sufficiently fast once the data is actually stored in memory. The main problems are those associated with data file handling especially when floppy discs are used. Experience has taught me that indexed sequential file organisation is very much a mixed blessing in microcomputer COBOL; in some circumstances it should be avoided if at all possible as it may provide the worst of all worlds rather than the best.

In this book I have tried to pass on to the reader some of the things I have learnt, sometimes painfully, in several years of using microcomputer COBOL. Let me emphasis that the book is not intended to teach the reader how to program. It is aimed at the reader who can program, or at least understands the processes involved in all programming, who wishes to learn about this popular language called COBOL as used on microcomputers. It is also aimed at the programmer experienced in mainframe versions of COBOL who is going over to program microcomputers.

Inevitably I owe a debt of gratitude to many people. In particular my thanks must go to colleagues at the Polytechnic of North London—to Dr Garry Marshall at whose suggestion this book was written and who has given me a great deal of advice and help and to Stan Buttimer for acting both as a sounding board for ideas and as a calming influence during some of the more frustrating periods of writing and compiling the material. Outside of the Polytechnic, thanks must go to Philip Chapman of Newnes Technical Books for giving me the opportunity of writing this, my first book. And last, but certainly not least, my wife Thelma for her unflagging support.

Norman Stang

Contents

1
Introduction to COBOL

History of COBOL

In the early days of computing, up to the late 1950s, the programmer had at his disposal, at best, assembly languages, which provided little more than mnemonic codes for machine language instructions. There was no standardisation of programming languages and little or no portability of programs even between different models of computer produced by the same manufacturer.

The prime mover behind attempts to standardise computer software was the US Department of Defense, which wished to protect its vast investment in computer programming effort by achieving a large element of machine-independence. The history of COBOL dates from May 1959 when a meeting was called by a Mr Charles Phillips of the Department of Defence at the Pentagon.

Present at the meeting were representatives of computer user installations (from both private and government sectors), universities, and computer manufacturers. At this meeting the Conference On Data Systems Langagues (CODASYL) was established and committees set up. The initial committee was composed of representatives from six computer manufacturers and three government agencies, including the National Bureau of Standards. In its specifications for the new language three purposes had to be met:

1. The language had to be machine-independent, in that the basic language elements had to be common to all computers.
2. The language as written by the programmer, the 'source' language, had to be easy to understand and use.
3. The language had to include business terminology, or at least cater for business terminology.

In April 1960 the first specification of the new language, COBOL 60 (COBOL standing for COmmon Business Oriented Language), was published. Each computer manufactuer was expected to make available a 'compiler', which translated a program written in

1

COBOL into the machine language of their particular computer. The initial specification was ambiguous and some compilers interpreted phrases differently from others. As a result, a COBOL maintenance committee was set up to clarify the language and, later, to extend the language and its facilities. By October 1960 two compilers had been released; and within five years some 70 COBOL compilers had been implemented throughout the world.

Unfortunately, the early compilers suffered from a number of snags. First, in general, only a small sub-set of the total language was implemented, and different compilers implemented different sub-sets, thus reducing compatibility. Secondly, compilation times tended to be long, particularly if the compiler implemented a large sub-set of the total language—anything up to an hour for a single program. Thirdly, the 'object' or machine code generated by early compilers was inefficient, typically requiring two to five times the memory space of an assembly language program written to perform the same functions.

The new generation of mainframe computers introduced in the mid 1960s, such as the IBM 360, heralded the era of 'upwards compatibility' within families of computers, thus enabling programs written for a smaller model in the 'family' to be run on a larger model. This was achieved at hardware level as well as software. But there was still only limited compatibility between computers from rival manufacturers, for not only did the different manufacturers choose different optional features for their versions of COBOL, but they also added their own extensions to the language to enable programmers to make use of particular facilities offered by the computer hardware, and to help tie the customer to that computer supplier.

To ensure continuity of communication between users and suppliers of COBOL, the American National Standards Institute (ANSI) has tried to encourage the standardisation of the language. ANSI also ensures that the standards are generally recognised and accepted, and represents US interests in international standardisation.

The importance of standards can be seen in the state of chaos which gave rise to the development of COBOL in the first place. Adherence to laid-down standards has helped to ensure the protection of investment in program writing and systems development even where the organisation has changed the hardware it used.

The current standard is the 1974 ANSI version, which even at its basic level is well able to meet the data processing needs of most small computer users. Only the large mainframe computers use versions of COBOL which include such features as Sort and Report Writer functions. There are proposals to extend the language to include teleprocessing and database processing; any such extensions would be incorporated in a new standard.

The Microcomputer

Microcomputers began to gain popularity in the mid 1970s. Compared to mainframe computers, these had little memory storage capacity and were physically small enough and cheap enough to attract the 'hobbyist'. They were based on newly developed microprocessors built on silicon chips, of which there were several competing varieties, the most popular being the Z80, 8080 and 6502.

Each of the rival chips had its proponents, many of whom programmed their microcomputers in assembly language. However, BASIC, a language initially developed for use on timesharing systems in colleges, was quickly established as the *de facto* standard high-level language, though there were several different dialects of the language in actual use. As a programming language, BASIC enjoyed the important advantages of being easy to learn and quick to write. But it did tend to suffer from four disadvantages which limited its potential as a business user's language:

1. It had not business or pseudo-business terminology, and the construction of the instruction set owned more to scientific application than to business.
2. Programs were often not easily transportable from one type of computer to another.
3. Communication between machine and user tended to be of a question/answer nature. This in part reflected the early history of BASIC and its use in conjunction with 'hard copy' teletype terminals installed in schools and colleges. Given that business users were more likely to use visual display units (VDUs), effective acceptable communications required the ability to format pseudo-documents on a screen, particularly for the input of data. Such an ability was beyond most versions of BASIC.
4. BASIC generally offered a limited range of file access/retrieval methods. Data files stored on direct access devices such as floppy disc were most easily stored and retrieved sequentially. Random retrieval of stored data from floppy disc involved devising algorithms which provided a pointer to the position of the required record relative to the beginning of the file. This was simple enough if records, such as those of customers, were numbered sequentially, 1, 2, 3, . . . In practice, file coding was rarely that simple and complex algorithms had sometimes to be constructed, with codes containing alphabetic characters presenting particular problems.

3

The business user and COBOL

So why should the business user choose COBOL in particular? The type of business most likely to consider the use of a microcomputer is probably a small concern with a small budget for data processing functions. In introducing a computer-based system, the company looks for such benefits as reduced staffing levels, greater accuracy and better statistical analysis.

Such businesses could not be expected to change their methods of operation completely. For example, the business holds files of customers, suppliers, products, etc, each of which has a unique identity or 'key'. Each business has its own unique coding system to identify individual customers, suppliers, etc. For example, the product code may be constructed from a number of factors reflecting perhaps raw materials used, or process paths to be followed, or dimensions. Most businesses are, quite naturally, unwilling to change their coding systems simply to meet the requirements of a computer system. Indeed, the reverse is true; the computer system introduced has to meet the requirements of the company.

The business user of a microcomputer has a smaller budget for all data processing functions than the user of a mainframe computer, with the programming costs accounting for a substantial part of the total cost of a system. If a company wishes to develop its own computer systems, it is easier and cheaper to employ an experienced COBOL programmer than a BASIC programmer if only because there are many more programmers experienced in the use of COBOL than in the use of BASIC. The cost of the programming function and the sheer availability of suitably experienced programmers cannot be too strongly emphasised. Further, insofar as non-computer personnel are involved in the systems analysis and design functions, they find it easier to understand programming functions expressed in business terms.

The requirements of another group of people must also be taken into account—the auditors. Increasingly, auditors have been coming to grips with the need to examine source code of the programs to ensure that procedures are correctly executed. Auditors are normally used to examining programs written in COBOL, and not in other languages. Many firms of auditors have prepared their own suites of programs and test data to test user systems. These have been written with COBOL programs in mind on the assumption that virtually all business users of computers use COBOL. And so COBOL scores over BASIC and other languages used in micro-computer systems on yet further grounds.

COBOL, as available on microcomputers, does not suffer from

4

some of the disadvantages that have been noted above in relation to BASIC. Versions of the language such as CIS COBOL have been specially designed to cater for the specific needs of microcomputer users. Take, for example the design of forms on the normal 80 column by 24 row VDU screen. Each of the 1920 character positions can be easily referenced by line number and position on the line. Characters may be displayed in any specified position on the screen; similarly data can be entered into the computer from any nominated position on the screen. Headings can be 'protected' so that they cannot be overwritten, while other screen positions, containing input data, can be 'permitted' so that they can be refreshed with new data. Microfocus, the producers of CIS COBOL, has also produced a software package, FORMS II, to facilitate the design and creation of pseudo-forms on the VDU screen.

COBOL provides indexed file organization as well as the sequential and relative file methods associated with BASIC. This enables files with complex keys to be accessed sequentially and/or randomly without the need to construct complex key transformation algorithms.

So COBOL provides a virtually complete programming system for the small business user who wishes to develop programs that can be easily used by VDU operators, whose main concern is to input data in as easy a manner as possible through manageable forms.

Microcomputer COBOL versus mainframe computer COBOL

The power and range of facilities provided by the versions of COBOL available depend upon the size and power of the computer used in compiling and running the programs.

Essentially the microcomputer versions contain all the major file formats and instructions. However, certain variations of instructions are omitted, though these tend to be the less used variants. Similarly, certain facilities which require major processing, such as sorting and merging and report writing, are available in mainframe versions of COBOL only at present. But report programs are relatively simple to write, and there are special purpose programs available to sort data files. Thus to the business microcomputer user COBOL is to be regarded as one of several pieces of software to be utilised rather than the total sum of software required.

Summary

This chapter has considered the development of COBOL as a programming language intended to meet the needs of business users.

Since its inception in 1960 it has become by far the most important commercial programming language for mainframe computer users.

The main appeal of COBOL has been the use of everyday English expressions and the ease of modification of source programs so that the same program could be run on different models of computer supplied by different manufacturers.

```
000100 IDENTIFICATION DIVISION.
000200 PROGRAM-ID.  LIST.
000300 ENVIRONMENT DIVISION.
000400 CONFIGURATION SECTION.
000500 SOURCE-COMPUTER. MODEL-XYZ.
000600 OBJECT-COMPUTER. MODEL-XYZ.
000700 INPUT-OUTPUT SECTION.
000800 FILE-CONTROL.
000900      SELECT PRODUCT-FILE ASSIGN TO "PRODUCT.DAT"
001000          ORGANIZATION IS INDEXED
001100          ACCESS MODE IS SEQUENTIAL
001200          RECORD KEY IS PRODUCT-NO.
001300      SELECT PRINT-FILE ASSIGN TO ":LP:".
001400 DATA DIVISION.
001500 FILE SECTION.
001600 FD  PRODUCT-FILE.
001700 01  PRODUCT-RECORD.
001800      02   PRODUCT-NO     PIC X(5).
001900      02   PRODUCT-DESC   PIC X(20).
002000      02   PRODUCT-PRICE  PIC 9(4)V99.
002100      02   PRODUCT-QTY    PIC 9(4).
002200      02   PRODUCT-YEAR   PIC 99.
002300      02   PRODUCT-MONTH  PIC 99.
002400      02   PRODUCT-DAY    PIC 99.
002500 FD  PRINT-FILE.
002600 01  PRINT-RECORD.
002700      02   FILLER         PIC X(4).
002800      02   PRINT-NO       PIC X(5).
002900      02   FILLER         PIC X(6).
003000      02   PRINT-DESC     PIC X(20).
003100      02   FILLER         PIC XXX.
003200      02   PRINT-PRICE    PIC Z(4).99.
003300      02   FILLER         PIC X(6).
003400      02   PRINT-QTY      PIC Z(4).
003500      02   FILLER         PIC XX.
003600      02   PRINT-VALUE    PIC ZZ,ZZZ,ZZZ.ZZ.
003700      02   FILLER         PIC XXX.
003800      02   PRINT-DAY      PIC 99.
003900      02   FILLER         PIC X.
004000      02   PRINT-MONTH    PIC 99.
004100      02   FILLER         PIC X.
004200      02   PRINT-YEAR     PIC 99.
004300      02   FILLER         PIC X.
004400*
004500 WORKING-STORAGE SECTION.
004600 01  LINE-COUNT    PIC 99    VALUE 99.
004700 01  HEAD-1        PIC X(46) VALUE
004800      "                         PRODUCT LIST".
004900 01  HEAD-2        PIC X(46) VALUE
005000      "                         ------------".
005100 01  HEAD-3        PIC X(82) VALUE
005200      "PRODUCT CODE    DESCRIPTION            UNIT PRICE    QUANTITY
005300-     "    VALUE    LAST MOVED".
005400*
005500*
```

Fig. 1.1 A COBOL program to print the contents of a file

To date, COBOL has not had the same success with micro-computer users as with mainframe computer users. But the superiority of data entry presentation and of file handling in microcomputer versions of COBOL as compared with BASIC look like establishing COBOL as a major language for business users of microcomputers.

As an illustration of a not untypical COBOL program the example program in Fig. 1.1 prints the contents of a file. The main features to note are the use of everyday words and the clear separation of the selection and description of data elements (lines 001600–005300) from instructions which manipulate the data (lines 010200–013400).

```
010000 PROCEDURE DIVISION.
010100 OPEN-FILES.
010200     OPEN INPUT PRODUCT-FILE
010300          OUTPUT PRINT-FILE.
010400 READ-DATA.
010500     READ PRODUCT-FILE AT END GO TO FINISH.
010600     IF LINE-COUNT < 57 GO TO MOVE-DATA.
010700*
010800*   Print headings at top of page
010900*
011000     MOVE SPACE TO PRINT-RECORD.
011100     WRITE PRINT-RECORD BEFORE ADVANCING PAGE.
011200     WRITE PRINT-RECORD FROM HEAD-1 BEFORE ADVANCING 1 LINE.
011300     WRITE PRINT-RECORD FROM HEAD-2 BEFORE ADVANCING 2 LINES.
011400     WRITE PRINT-RECORD FROM HEAD-3 BEFORE ADVANCING 2 LINES.
011500     MOVE SPACE TO PRINT-RECORD.
011600     MOVE 5 TO LINE-COUNT.
011700*
011800 MOVE-DATA.
011900     MOVE PRODUCT-NO TO PRINT-NO.
012000     MOVE PRODUCT-DESC TO PRINT-DESC.
012100     MOVE PRODUCT-PRICE TO PRINT-PRICE.
012200     MOVE PRODUCT-QTY TO PRINT-QTY.
012300     MULTIPLY PRODUCT-PRICE BY PRODUCT-QTY GIVING PRINT-VALUE.
012400     MOVE PRODUCT-DAY TO PRINT-DAY.
012500     MOVE PRODUCT-MONTH TO PRINT-MONTH.
012600     MOVE PRODUCT-YEAR TO PRINT-YEAR.
012700     WRITE PRINT-RECORD BEFORE ADVANCING 1 LINE.
012800     MOVE SPACE TO PRINT-RECORD.
012900     ADD 1 TO LINE-COUNT.
013000     GO TO READ-DATA.
013100*
013200 FINISH.
013300     WRITE PRINT-RECORD BEFORE ADVANCING PAGE.
013400     CLOSE PRODUCT-FILE PRINT-FILE.
013500     STOP RUN.
```

Fig. 1.1 Cont.

2

The microcomputer environment

As mentioned in the previous chapter, the program as written by the programmer is known as the source program and is written, as far as we are concerned, in the language known as COBOL. On micro-computers, the source program is written onto a floppy disc by means of a program known as a text editor or by means of a word processing program. The source program is stored on the disc as a file.

The operating system

The storage of files is controlled by the 'operating system', a master control program. Different types of microcomputer use different operating systems. However, at present, the one most commonly used is known as CP/M (Control Program Monitor). Operating systems tend to be similar in terms of the functions they perform, though the actual instructions used may vary.

In view of its common use, we shall be looking at CP/M as a typical operating system. As a control program CP/M performs two major functions: the maintenance of files on discs and the handling of communications with the VDU operator. Much of this communication relates to files.

Maintenance of files

File maintenance is achieved through the maintenance of a directory of named files. This director contains the names of the files and information about which sectors on the disc contain the data which makes up the files.

The user is freed from many of the file creation and file mainte-nance housekeeping requirements often associated with mainframe computers.

Communication with the user

Once loaded into the microcomputer's random access memory (RAM), CP/M can be given two types of commands, known as built-in and transient commands.

Both types of commands are generally associated with file, or file directory, handling or maintenance. These commands will be considered further later in the chapter.

Loading CP/M and systems prompts

The precise method of loading CP/M into RAM will vary from one microcomputer to another, and so it will be necessary, in practice, to follow the start-up instructions supplied with the micromputer.

When CP/M is loaded it sends a message to that effect back to the VDU. This message is known as a 'systems prompt' and normally takes the form

A>

The A indicates that disc drive A is the one which is currently selected or logged and is thus the control disc.

In a system with two or more disc drives, control may be passed to another drive by typing in the drive identification letter followed by colon. Thus

B:

will cause control to pass to drive B. The system should then repond with

B>

as the new systems prompt.

The significance of the drive number in the systems prompt will begin to emerge when we consider file names and file handling commands in CP/M.

File names

The CP/M system allows the user considerable freedom in the assigning of names to files. The file has a two part description. The first part is the file name. This must be composed of between one and eight characters, generally, but not necessarily, alphabetic or numeric. The name may be followed by a full stop and a three-character extension. The use of file extensions by the user is

9

optional, though the software may require or use certain extensions.

The user may choose any name and extension for data files. For example

ABC
STAN1
PRODUCT.DAT
SOFTWARE.TXT

are all valid file descriptions.

As most software may require the use of or may create particular extensions, it would be wise to follow conventional usage as far as extensions are concerned. Among the more commonly used extensions are

BAK (used by several text editing and word processing programs as the extension for backup, or security, copies of text)

BAS (used as the source program extension by the CBASIC compiler system)

COM (the commonly used extension for systems programs)

IDX (used by CIS COBOL as the index part of an index file)

INT (used as the extension for the object or machine language version of CBASIC and COBOL programs)

PRT (commonly used as the extension for print-image files)

This list is not exhaustive by any means, and it would be prudent to stick to extensions such as DAT for data files and CBL for the source version of COBOL programs. Equally, it makes sense to use meaningful file names. For example, PRODUCT.DAT is more self-explanatory than BONK.ZZZ.

A complete file specification would include the disc drive designation, which is a letter followed by a colon. Thus

A:PRODUCT.DAT

refers to the file PRODUCT.DAT which is to be found on the disc in drive A.

If the disc designation is not cited, then the system will look for the file on the currently logged disc. Thus, if the COBOL program contained the instruction

SELECT ORDER-FILE ASSIGN TO "ORDERS.DAT"
    ORGANIZATION IS SEQUENTIAL.

the system would look for the file ORDERS.DAT on the disc that was logged or selected at the time the program was loaded. But the COBOL instruction

SELECT ORDERS-FILE ASSIGN TO "B:ORDERS.DAT"
ORGANIZATIONAL IS SEQUENTIAL

would cause the system to look for the file specifically on disc drive B.

There are two useful 'wild' characters '?' and '*', that may be used in file references when used in CP/M built-in and transient commands. These characters have specified meanings.

The '?' means any character in the position occupied by the ?. For example, suppose a disc contains the following files

ORDERS.DAT
ORDER1.DAT
ORDER2.DAT
ORDER15.DAT

A command to ORDERS.DAT will refer to that file only. But a command to ORDER?.DAT will refer to all files which have names six characters long, the first five of which are ORDER. In this example, ORDERS.DAT ORDER1.DAT and ORDER2.DAT are processed; ORDER15.DAT is not.

The '*' will cause the system to process in built-in and transient commands all file names and/or extensions which are common. For example, suppose the disc contains the following files

ORDERS.DAT
PRODUCT.DAT
PRODUCT.IDX
PRODUCT

a command which references PRODUCT.* will act upon all files with the name PRODUCT, whatever the extension. Thus a command specifying PRODUCT.* will cause PRODUCT.DAT, PRODUCT.IDX and PRODUCT all to be processed.

Built-in commands

Built-in commands are intrinsic to CP/M itself. As far as the COBOL user is concerned there are four major built-in commands, all of which are concerned with files or with the file directory. They are DIR, ERA, REN and TYPE.

The DIR command asks for the file directory to be listed on the VDU. An example is shown in Fig. 2.1. The format of the command is simply

DIR

A:	MOVCPM/M	COM	MOVCPM/D	COM	MOVCPM/S	COM	SYSGEN	COM
A:	SUBMIT	COM	XSUB	COM	MBASIC4	COM	MBASIC5	COM
A:	SC	COM	ZSM	COM	RAID	COM	POOLS	INT
A:	LOAD	COM	DUMP	COM	MULT	INT	MULT	BAS
A:	FORMAT/8	COM	BIO	INT	BACKUP/8	COM	BIO	CBL
A:	SORT	COM	MAP	COM	WORM	COM	FLASH11	COM
A:	MDIAG	COM	COBOL	COM	GUIDE	WS	POOLS	BAS
A:	DUMP	HEX	DUMP	PRN	CBAS2	COM	CRUN2	COM
A:	COBOL	OV1	MAXPRO	INT	MAXPRO	BAS	COBOL	OV2
A:	FRED	DDS	TEST1	INT	COBOL	OV3	COBOL	OV4
A:	TEST1	CBL	BIO	BAS	TEST3	INT	TEST3	CBL
A:	INSTALL	COM	RUN	COM	CONFIG	COM	ELAST	BAS
A:	ELAST	INT	T-COM4	COM	R-COM4	COM	FORMS2	INT
A:	FACT	WS	FORMS2	I01	FORMS2	I02	FORMS2	W01
A:	FORMS2	W02	FORMS2	H01	FORMS2	H02	FORMS2	H03
A:	FORMS2	H04	FORMS2	CH1	FORMS2	GN1	FORMS2	GN2
A:	FORMS2	CH2	FORMS2	COM	QPARM	BAS	QSORT	COM
A:	QPARM	INT	FRED	CHK	TEST2	CBL	TEST2	INT
A:	CONFIG/8	COM						

Fig. 2.1 An example of a file directory listing, following a DIR command

It is possible to command the system to produce a listing of the file directory of the non-currently selected disc. If disc drive A is currently selected,

DIR B:

will list the directory of the disc on drive B.

A more limited file directory listing can be obtained. For example

DIR *.COM

will list all files which have the extension COM.

The ERA command is used to erase a file or group of files from the disc. The file names are removed from the file directory and the disc space they had previously occupied is freed for use by new files.

To erase a single file called CUST.DAT on the current drive we would enter

ERA CUST.DAT

To erase all files on disc B which have the name PRODUCT (with or without any extension) we would enter

ERA B:PRODUCT.*

Equally, we may wish to remove all files with a particular extension (such as INT) from the disc in the current drive. To do so we would enter

ERA *.INT

The REN command is used to rename a file. The effect modifies

12

the file directory so that the file is known by its new name. For example,

    REN HISTORY.DAT=INVOICE.DAT

results in the file previously known to the system as INVOICE.DAT being renamed HISTORY.DAT. The data which constitutes the file is unchanged; the file cannot be transferred to another disc by means of the rename command.

    The TYPE command is used to obtain a listing of the contents of any file. The listing is displayed on the VDU screen. The format of a typical command is

    TYPE PRODUCT.DAT

which will result in the contents of PRODUCT.DAT being displayed on the screen in the sequence in which the data file is stored. A typical listing is shown in Fig. 2.2.

Transient commands

Transient commands are carried out by calling and executing a utility program. COBOL users will normally require just two of CP/M's utility programs, PIP and STAT.

    PIP stands for Peripheral Interchange Program—a utility used to transfer files from one disc to another, though it can transfer information to other devices such as printers. PIP is an extremely useful program which enables security copies of both programs and data files to be made.

    There are various options available. The major ones are:

    (i) copy the contents of the file onto another on the same disc. For example

    PIP HISTORY.DAT=INFOR.DAT

In this case a new file, HISTORY.DAT, is created on the same disc as INFO.DAT and will contain the same data. The original file remains unaltered.

    (ii) copy the contents of one file to another file on another disc with the same file name. For example

    PIP B:PRODUCT.DAT=A:PRODUCT.DAT

will cause a file PRODUCT.DAT to be created or overwritten with the contents of the file PRODUCT.DAT currently held on disc A. In other words, both discs will contain the same file names and file data contents. The same effect can be achieved by means of the shorter command.

```
BI569RALEIGH BOXER          0080000020830216
BI591RALEIGH STRIKA         0065000015830216
BI597TRIKE TRIPPER          0019990021830216
BI612VIVA CIRCUS            0034990009830216
BI614RODEA                  0035000010830216
BI615RALEIGH SMALL RIDER    0055000012830216
BI617VISCOUNT POLO          0056750012830216
BI618VISCOUNT SPRINT        0095000015830216
BI641MARLBORO COUNTESS      0110000012830316
BI642MARLBORO OMEGA 20      0099990012830316
BI643EAGLE 12               0023500013830216
BI644VIVA DEBBIE            0047500014830216
BI645VIVA TRACKSTAR         0055000015830216
BI646VISCOUNT JR SPORT      0097500015830316
BI651BMX FIREBALLER         0085000012830316
BI652RALEIGH GRIFTER        0085000013830316
BI656RALEIGH TOUR DE FR.    0122500005830316
BI659RALEIGH VICTORIA       0100050000830316
BI661RALEIGH SHOPPER        0099990010830316
BI662RALEIGH GRANADA        0094950014830316
BI666RALEIGH JAVELIN        0095500010830316
BI670RALEIGH WEEKENDER      0119990012830316
BI673RALEIGH PRIMA          0159500016830316
BI677RALEIGH BOMBER         0085000020830316
BI678MARLBORO CAVALIER      0110000021830316
BI683RALEIGH FOLDER         0075000017830316
CA004GAZ LUMOGAZ            0017990124820517
CA019GAZ BLEUET S200 STOV0011550175820517
CA057COOKWARE SET - SATIN0014990036820517
CA058COOKWARE SET - RED     0016990014820517
CA074INSULATED FOOD JAR     0008990001820517
CA075INSULATED JUG          0007990013820517
CA078CAMPARI COMB. KNIFE 0006250387820517
CA502CAMP BED               0010990024820517
CA509HIBACHI DB BARBECUE 0007750075820517
CA511HAGO ELPEY TWIN BURN0039990014820517
CA513TILLEY TRIPLE BURNER0036950017820517
CA517TILLEY STORM LANTERN0029950006820517
CA827TILLEY TALISMAN STOV0049950014820517
CA850LOUNGER                0014990018820517
CA855SLEEPING BAG 26 OZ     0010990104820517
CA856SLEEPING BAG 38 OX     0011990048820517
CA857SLEEPING BAG 44 OZ     0014990000820517
CA868CURVER COOL BOX 17 L0009990144820517
CA869CURVER COOL BOC 25 L0011990048820517
CA870CURVER COOL BOX 36 L0017990024820517
CA872INSULATED COOL BAG     0005500009820517
CA873PICNIC HAMPER          0038990004820517
CA875FOLDING TABLE - SING0010990004820517
CA876FOLDING TABLE - DB     0021990003820517
CL516HOOVER FREEDOM 750     0049990012830316
CL526HOOVER CELEBRITY       0059990013830316
CL559GOBLIN CYLINDER        0038750018830316
CL562ELECTROLUX 355         0089500C13830316
CL567MOULINEX  MAJOR        0079990018830316
CL569ELECTROLUX 5025        0089950020830316
CL571HOTPOINT UNIVERSAL     0099950013830316
CL577HOOVER FREEDOM 1000 0069950020830316
CL582HOOVER JUNIOR          0072500015830316
```

Fig. 2.2 A typical file listing as a result of a TYPE command

14

PIP B:=A:PRODUCT.DAT.

(iii) copy all files with a particular name (and any extension) to another disc. For example

PIP B:=A:PRODUCT.*

(iv) copy all files with a particular extension (whatever the name) to another disc. For example

PIP A:=B:*.INT

would copy all files on disc B with the extension INT to disc drive A.

(v) copy all files from one disc to another. For example

PIP B:=A:*.*

would copy all files from disc A to disc B.

There are other PIP options available, and these are explained in the CP/M users' guide.

The STAT utility program lets the user see various disc utilisation statistics, and may allow some characteristics to be changed. Options available include:

(i) finding out how much disc space is available. This is achieved through entering the command STAT as shown in Fig. 2.3.

```
A>STAT
A: R/W, Space: 52k
```

Fig.2.3 Ascertaining available disc space with the command STAT

(ii) finding out how much disc space is occupied by various files. An example is shown in Fig. 2.4.

```
A>STAT *.CBL

Recs   Bytes   Ext  Acc
  98    16k      1  R/W  A:BIO.CBL
  21     4k      1  R/W  A:FIG151.CBL
   7     4k      1  R/W  A:FIG152.CBL
  10     4k      1  R/W  A:FIG71.CBL
  11     4k      1  R/W  A:FIG74.CBL
  27     4k      1  R/W  A:LIST.CBL
   9     4k      1  R/W  A:LOAD.CBL
   8     4k      1  R/W  A:START.CBL
   7     4k      1  R/W  A:TEST1.CBL
   7     4k      1  R/W  A:TEST2.CBL
   6     4k      1  R/W  A:TEST3.CBL
   9     4k      1  R/W  A:UNLOAD.CBL
  60     8k      1  R/W  A:UPDT.CBL
Bytes Remaining On A: 20k
```

Fig. 2.4 Another use of the STAT command

(iii) setting a drive to read-only (writing to the disc drive would not be permitted by the system) through

STAT B:=R/O

(iv) setting a file to read-only through a command such as

STAT PRODUCT.DAT $R/O

Writing COBOL source programs

A COBOL source program may be considered as a piece of text, with each line in the program ending with a carriage return/line feed.

The program listed in the previous chapter was entered by means of the Wordstar word processing package, which is far easier to use for entry and modification of source programs than CP/M's context editor, ED. Wordstar recognises two types of text: a document file which has a line length fixed at virtually any number of character, but with the carriage return at the end of the paragraph; and a non-document file of variable line length, each line ending with carriage return/line feed.

COBOL source programs should be entered in such systems as non-document files. As each character is entered, the column number at the head of the screen is updated to show the current position of the cursor. This enables the person entering the program to ensure that code is written starting in the appropriate part of the coding form.

Cursor control is possible through the use of the control key simultaneously with alphabetic keys. This enables the user to insert missing text and delete unwanted text. Wordstar, and any other good word processing system for that matter, is menu driven with 'help' screens to assist the user as far as possible.

One facility which should *not* be used is the 'tab' key, or equivalent, to move the cursor from the end of the program line number (column 6 of a COBOL program) to the text area (normally column 12). This is because a spurious character will be inserted that is not acceptable to the compiler.

COBOL statements may be entered up to and including column 72, but it is recommended that for purposes of clarity there should not be more than one statement per line of text.

COBOL programs as files

A COBOL program is a file like any other. By the use of built-in and transient commands it can be copied, renamed, listed and erased. However, the source program cannot be run; it needs to be compiled or translated into 'object' or machine language form.

The precise instructions to compile a COBOL program will vary according to the compiler used. The method used to compile CIS COBOL programs is quite typical of the method normally to be found. This is:

(a) to instruct that a certain named source program is to be compiled;
(b) that the object version of the program is to be placed on a certain specified disc;
(c) that a listing of the source program and any errors found during compilation be suppressed, or listed on the printer, or put into a print-image file on disc for subsequent printing.

For example, to compile the source program LIST.CBL we might give the command

COBOL LIST.CBL

This is the minimum command, and the compiler will operate assuming various default values. In this case, the source program, LIST.CBL, will be compiled and the object version, LIST.INT, created onto the currently selected disc. A print-image version of the program listing, LIST.PRT, is put onto the same disc and may be printed later.

By contrast,

COBOL LIST.CBL INT(B:REPORT.INT) LIST(:LP:)

will compile the source program LIST.CBL, create an object version called REPORT.INT onto disc B, and print a listing of the source program at the time of compilation directly on the printer.

The object version of a COBOL program has the extension INT. Like the source version it can be copied, renamed and erased. It cannot be listed.

Storage of source and object programs

Source programs, their object versions, and data files may all be stored on the same disc. Precisely how many programs and how many files may be stored on a single disc will depend upon two main factors: the storage requirements of each file, and the storage capacity of the disc itself.

17

For security purposes it is worth organizing programs and data files in a way that facilitates ease of systems maintenance and does not cause a risk of running out of disc storage space. Thus it is worth keeping source and object versions of programs on separate discs. The source program, once correct, may not require frequent amendment and need only be accessed when making amendments through, perhaps, legislative requirements. On a day-to-day basis the source version is not required.

The object version, on the other hand, is required in order to run the program. It is therefore to be regarded as part of the everyday operating software and will probably be held on the same disc as the operating system and other object programs required in the execution of a job.

Data files may be stored on the same disc as the operating software if there is adequate space, but it may make better sense to keep data files on separate discs from the object programs.

Summary

This chapter has described the nature of COBOL programs as source programs written in COBOL language and object programs in machine language.

Programs are run in the environment set by the operating system, which is concerned primarily with the functions of file maintenance and the handling of communications with the VDU operator. The way in which one major operating system (CP/M) carries out these functions was examined as was the place of COBOL programs in the operating system environment.

Self-test questions

1 Write the CP/M commands to:
   (a) change the selected disc from A to B;
   (b) transfer the data file CUST.DAT from disc A to B, giving the version on disc B the name OLDCUST.DAT;
   (c) rename CUST.DAT on disc A as CUST1.DAT;
   (d) see how much disc space on B is occupied by all files with the extension INT.

2 What is a transient command?

3
The structure of a COBOL program

The COBOL language is structured in such a way that the program is a self-contained unit that describes all the data to be processed, followed by the instructions required for handling and manipulating the data.

Data is of two types: files and working storage.

Files

A file can be defined as a group of data records that are stored and processed together as a unit.

The storage of data files is external to the computer itself, and is normally on magnetic disc. The disc, as mentioned in the previous chapter, may hold many files.

Each record in a computer file is similar in size and structure in that the records are composed of fields of sizes and the sequence specified by the programmer, each field containing a specific element of information such as a customer account number or a name. An example of a layout is shown in Fig. 3.1.

COBOL files may also be files printed on paper, most commonly called reports. The format of the report normally shows the data presented in tabulations, with each line containing a number of specified items of information. A sample report is shown in Fig. 3.2.

It should be noted that microcomputer versions of COBOL are

PRODUCT CODE	5 CHARACTERS (1-2 ALPHA, 3-5 NUMERIC)
DESCRIPTION	20 CHARACTERS
PRICE	6 CHARACTERS (££££pp)
QUANTITY	4 CHARACTERS
DATE	6 CHARACTERS (YYMMDD)

Fig. 3.1 File layout of a product file

PRODUCT CODE	DESCRIPTION	UNIT PRICE	QUANTITY	VALUE	LAST MOVED
BI569	RALEIGH BOXER	80.00	20	1,600.00	16 02 83
BI591	RALEIGH STRIKA	65.00	15	975.00	16 02 83
BI597	TRIKE TRIPPER	19.99	21	419.79	16 02 83
BI612	VIVA CIRCUS	34.99	9	314.91	16 02 83
BI614	RODEA	35.00	10	350.00	16 02 83
BI615	RALEIGH SMALL RIDER	55.00	12	6C3.00	16 02 83
BI617	VISCOUNT POLO	56.75	12	681.00	16 02 83
BI618	VISCOUNT SPRINT	95.00	15	1,425.00	16 02 83
BI641	MARLBORO COUNTESS	110.00	12	1,320.00	16 03 83
BI642	MARLBORO OMEGA 20	99.99	12	1,199.88	16 03 83
BI643	EAGLE 12	23.50	13	305.50	16 02 83
BI644	VIVA DEBBIE	47.50	14	665.00	16 02 83
BI645	VIVA TRACKSTAR	55.00	15	825.00	16 02 83
BI646	VISCOUNT JR SPORT	97.50	15	1,462.50	16 03 83
BI651	BMX FIREBALLER	85.00	12	1,020.00	16 03 83
BI652	RALEIGH GRIFTER	85.00	13	1,105.00	16 03 83
BI656	RALEIGH TOUR DE FR.	122.50	5	612.50	16 03 83
BI659	RALEIGH VICTORIA	100.05			16 03 83
BI661	RALEIGH SHOPPER	99.99	10	999.90	16 03 83
BI662	RALEIGH GRANADA	94.95	14	1,329.30	16 03 83
BI666	RALEIGH JAVELIN	95.50	10	955.00	16 03 83
BI670	RALEIGH WEEKENDER	119.99	12	1,439.88	16 03 83
BI673	RALEIGH PRIMA	159.50	16	2,552.00	16 03 83
BI677	RALEIGH BOMBER	85.00	20	1,700.00	16 03 83
BI678	MARLBORO CAVALIER	110.00	21	2,310.00	16 03 83
BI683	RALEIGH FOLDER	75.00	17	1,275.00	16 03 83
BS001	TIZER	.13	24	3.12	10 03 83
CA004	GAZ LUMOGAZ	17.99	124	2,230.76	17 05 82
CA019	GAZ BLEUET S200 STOV	11.55	175	2,021.25	17 05 82
CA057	COOKWARE SET - SATIN	14.99	36	539.64	17 05 82
CA058	COOKWARE SET - RED	16.99	14	237.86	17 05 82
CA074	INSULATED FOOD JAR	8.99	1	8.99	17 05 82
CA075	INSULATED JUG	7.99	13	103.87	17 05 82
CA078	CAMPARI COMB. KNIFE	6.25	387	2,418.75	17 05 82
CA502	CAMP BED	10.99	24	263.76	17 05 82
CA509	HIBACHI DB BARBECUE	7.75	75	581.25	17 05 82
CA511	HAGO ELPEY TWIN BURN	39.99	14	559.86	17 05 82
CA513	TILLEY TRIPLE BURNER	36.95	17	628.15	17 05 82
CA517	TILLEY STORM LANTERN	29.95	6	179.70	17 05 82
CA827	TILLEY TALISMAN STOV	49.95	14	699.30	17 05 82
CA850	LOUNGER	14.99	18	269.82	17 05 82
CA855	SLEEPING BAG 26 OZ	10.99	104	1,142.96	17 05 82
CA856	SLEEPING BAG 38 OX	11.99	48	575.52	17 05 82
CA857	SLEEPING BAG 44 OZ	14.99			17 05 82
CA868	CURVER COOL BOX 17 L	9.99	144	1,438.56	17 05 82
CA869	CURVER COOL BOC 25 L	11.99	48	575.52	17 05 82
CA870	CURVER COOL BOX 36 L	17.99	24	431.76	17 05 82
CA872	INSULATED COOL BAG	5.50	9	49.50	17 05 82
CA873	PICNIC HAMPER	38.99	4	155.96	17 05 82
CA875	FOLDING TABLE - SING	10.99	4	43.96	17 05 82
CA876	FOLDING TABLE - DB	21.99	3	65.97	17 05 82
CL516	HOOVER FREEDOM 750	49.99	12	599.88	16 03 83

Fig. 3.2 Sample printout

designed to hold files on disc and paper; they do not allow for the use of cassette tapes as a medium for file storage.

Essentially, COBOL file records are fixed in length in that each record in a file is of the same length. CP/M works to a disc record size of 128 characters, but COBOL permits data records of any length. The run-time monitor is responsible for controlling the transfer of data between disc and memory storage. Printer records may be up to 132 characters in length.

20

Working-storage data

While the COBOL program is very much concerned with the need to process data stored on files, it also needs to use other areas of storage to hold non-file, or working-storage, data. Examples of such working-storage data are headings, totals, tables, switches, and information communicated between the VDU operator and the computer.

These data elements form part of the data structure of the program, but their contents are stored in memory and not on an external storage medium and they may be changed during the execution of the program. Thus values in working-storage areas are transient.

Program structure

A COBOL program is structured as shown in Fig. 3.3. This clear hierarchical structure is shown more formally in the example given in Fig. 3.4.

Division structure

Every COBOL program consists of four Divisions, each of which

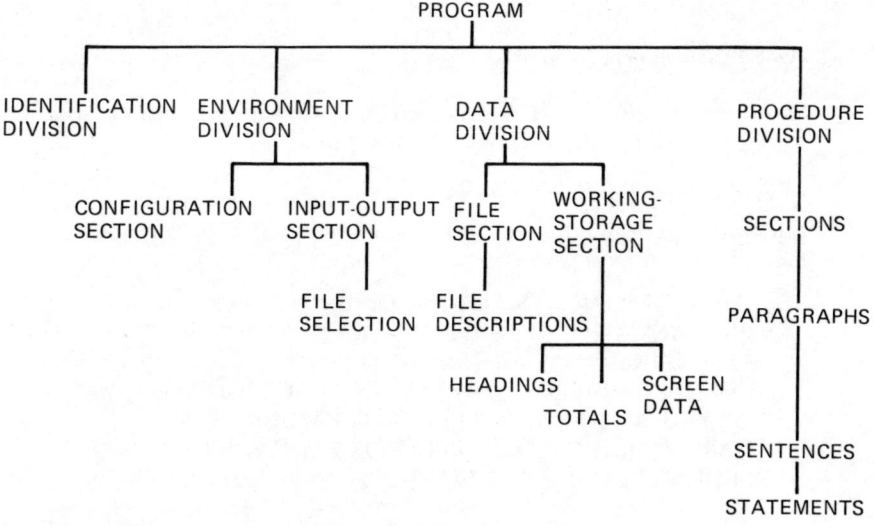

Fig. 3.3 The structure of a COBOL program

```
IDENTIFICATION DIVISION.
PROGRAM-ID.    program name.
ENVIRONMENT DIVISION.
CONFIGURATION SECTION.
SOURCE-COMPUTER.    computer type.
OBJECT-COMPUTER.    computer type.
INPUT-OUTPUT SECTION.
FILE-CONTROL.    file selection statements.
DATA DIVISION.
FILE SECTION.    file definitions
                 record definitions
WORKING-STORAGE SECTION.
                 work area definitions.

PROCEDURE DIVISION.
paragraph-name-1.
          procedures.

paragraph-name-2.
          procedures.

paragraph-name-3.
          procedures.

               .
               .
               .
```

Fig. 3.4 Example of program structure

has a distinct purpose. The program entries for each Divisions start with a line containing just the Division Name.

1. IDENTIFICATION DIVISION serves to provide the program with a unique identity and may include other, optional, documentation. For example.

```
IDENTIFICATION DIVISION
PROGRAM-ID.       UPDT.
AUTHOR.           N STANG.
INSTALLATION.     ABC MANUFACTURING.
DATE-WRITTEN.     11TH NOVEMBER 1982.
DATE-COMPILED.    17TH NOVEMBER 1982.
SECURITY.         NONE.
```

2. ENVIRONMENT DIVISION specifies the environment in

which the program is initially compiled and subsequently executed. In particular, it is used to specify:

(a) whether there is to be any interactive processing;
(b) whether special debugging facilities are to be included; and
(c) the names of the files to be processed by the program.

For example

```
ENVIRONMENT DIVISION.
CONFIGURATION SECTION.
SOURCE-COMPUTER.  MODEL-XYZ.
OBJECT-COMPUTER.  MODEL-XYZ MEMORY SIZE
     60000 CHARACTERS.
SPECIAL-NAMES.        CONSOLE IS CRT.
INPUT-OUTPUT SECTION.
FILE-CONTROL.
   SELECT   PRODUCT-FILE
     ASSIGN TO "PRODUCT.DAT"
     ORGANIZATION IS INDEXED
     ACCESS MODE IS SEQUENTIAL
     RECORD KEY IS PRODUCT-NO.
   SELECT PRINT-FILE ASSIGN TO ":LP:".
```

3. DATA DIVISION contains the data variables. These are:
(1) a detailed description of the files named in the INPUT-OUTPUT SECTION of the ENVIRONMENT DIVISION; for example

```
FD   PRODUCT-FILE
     PRODUCT-RECORD.
     02   PRODUCT-NO      PIC X(5)
     02   PRODUCT-DESC    PIC X(20).
     02   PRODUCT-PRICE   PIC 9(4)V99.
     02   PRODUCT-QTY     PIC 9(4).
     02   PRODUCT-DATE    PIC 9(6).
```

and

(b) the names and associated descriptive details of the working-storage data elements; for example

```
WORKING-STORAGE   SECTION
77   LINE-COUNT       PIC 99.
77   HEAD-1           PIC X(46) VALUE
       "                   PRODUCT LIST".
```

4. PROCEDURE DIVISION contains the procedural elements, or instructions, which manipulate the data defined in the DATA DIVISION.

Sections

With the exception of the IDENTIFICATION DIVISION, divisions may be subdivided into logical sections as follows.

The ENVIRONMENT DIVISION is composed of two sections:

(a) CONFIGURATION SECTION, which is used to specify the computer equipment used in compiling and running the program;
(b) INPUT-OUTPUT SECTION, which is used to specify the files to be processed.

The DATA DIVISION is normally composed of two sections:

(a) FILE SECTION, which as the name implies, is concerned with definitions of files;
(b) WORKING-STORAGE SECTION, which is used to define and describe non-file data.

It may also contain a LINKAGE SECTION to provide a data link between programs, where a master program may call into storage another program to be executed before having control returned to the master program.

The PROCEDURE DIVISION may, but need not, be subdivided into sections. It will, however, always contain named paragraphs. Whether sections are used will normally depend upon the programming standards adopted by the programmer; but the use of sections is often recommended when the program can be easily divided into distinct functional procedures, and the use of sections helps to make the program more comprehensible.

PROCEDURE DIVISION sections will be used where the program in total is so large that it cannot be completely accommodated in the computer's memory at execution time. The program will be divided into segments, each of which will contain one or more sections. The segments may be called into memory as required, overlaying other segments not needed at the time. The procedures involved in segmentation are explained further in Chapter 14.

Note that the COBOL language provides specific, compulsory,

section names and paragraph names in the ENVIRONMENT DIVISION and the DATA DIVISION. By contrast, the names given to sections and paragraphs in the PROCEDURE DIVISION are programmer-defined. That is, it is up to the programmer to decide on the actual names to be used. Different programmers write to different standards, but clarity would perhaps dictate the use of meaningful paragraph and section names in the PROCEDURE DIVISION.

The COBOL word

Broadly speaking, a program written in the COBOL language is made up from reserved words, programmer-defined words, and literals.

Reserved words

These are words which have specific meanings in the COBOL language. There are about 400 which are common to all versions of the language. In addition, each version of COBOL has a few non-standard reserved words.

Reserved words fall into the following categories:

(i) Keywords, which must be used in the appropriate place in the source program. Thus the very first line of a COBOL program consists of the two keywords IDENTIFICATION DIVISION. Procedure Division verbs such as ADD, SUBTRACT, READ, WRITE and so on are also keywords, as are certain required words which help to improve the readability of the program—words such as TO.

(ii) optional words, which are used only to make the program more comprehensible, and whose use is at the programmer's discretion. The word IS is an example of an optional word.

(iii) figurative constants, which are used to name and reference specific values. These are:

ZERO	which represents the value zero in the relevant
ZEROS	context.
ZEROES	

SPACE	which represents one or more of the character
SPACES	'space'.

QUOTE	which represents the double quotation
QUOTES	mark. There is need for this figurative constant because the double quotation mark itself has a specific use as a marker to delimit a non-numeric literal.
HIGH-VALUE	which represents one or more of the highest value in the computer's collating sequence. This is a value of all 1 bits in a character.
HIGH-VALUES	
LOW-VALUE	which represents one or more of the lowest value in the computer's collating sequence. This is a value of all 0 bits in a character.
LOW-VALUES	
ALL literal	represents the condition whereby the whole value is set to the literal value following the word ALL. Thus a field set to ALL "A" will result in having every character in the field set to 'A'.

(iv) special-character words. These are single characters which have specific meanings such as

= (equals)   > (greater than)   < (less than)

Programmer-defined words

These are words which are defined by the programmer. The most common use of the programmer-defined word is the data name defined by the programmer in the DATA DIVISION.

A typical COBOL Procedure Division statement might read

ADD COMMISSION TO TOTAL-VALUE.

The words ADD and TO are keywords, that is they must be used if the intention is to add two values together. But COMMISSION and TOTAL-VALUE are examples of the programmer-defined data names. The program will known which positions in memory are meant by COMMISSION and TOTAL-VALUE because the programmer will have declared those names in the DATA DIVISION, and will also have defined their sizes and characteristics.

The programmer will also declare section names and paragraph names in the PROCEDURE DIVISION.

The rules for making up a programmer-defined word are quite simple. They are:

(i) the word must not exceed 30 characters
(ii) the word must be composed from any of the following characters:

```
A B C . . . X Y Z
a b c . . . x y z
1 2 3 . . . 7 8 9
- (hyphen)
```

(iii) the word must neither start nor end with a hyphen
(iv) a data name must contain at least one alphabetic character.

COMMISSION PARAGRAPH-TO-PRINT-ADDRESSES and OVERTIME-1 are thus all valid programmer-defined words; 21 is a valid Procedure Division paragraph name or section name, but an invalid data name; -GROSS is an invalid programmer-defined word.

There is much disagreement in the programming world about how programmers ought to construct programmer-defined words. The rules governing what is allowed are simple and straightforward, as we have seen, but it is technically possible to construct programmer-defined words which are completely meaningless. The best rule to follow is to use meaningful words, so long as they are permissible, and generally try to avoid all but the most acceptable abbreviations. Good programming requires that the program is reasonably easy to understand, and this is aided by the use of meaningful programmer-defined words.

Literals

A literal is a group of characters which the computer recognises as being of a 'literal' or actual value. There are two types of literal:
(i) The numeric literal is a number whcih may be up to 18 digits in length. It may contain any numeral, a decimal point and a + or − sign.

Thus we might find a COBOL instruction which reads

ADD 24 TO TOTAL.

The value 24 is a numeric literal. (TOTAL is, of course, a programmer-defined data name.)

There are a few simple rules governing the construction of

numeric literals. These are commonsense and follow conventional usage of such values.

There may be only one sign character and this must appear at the left-hand end of the literal. Thus

> + 123 is a valid literal, whereas
> + − and 123 + are invalid.

There may be one, and only one, decimal point in a numerical literal, and this must not appear as the rightmost character. Thus

> 17.2 and .123 are valid
> 17..2 1.2.3 and 678. are invalid.

(ii) A non-numeric literal is a group of up to 128 characters, bounded at both ends by double quotation marks. The non-numeric literal may contain any allowable character from the computer's character set.

Thus we might use the instruction

> MOVE "** PRODUCT NOT ON FILE **" TO
> ERROR-MESSAGE.

But note that COBOL will not allow non-numeric literals to be used in arithmetic statements. For example, COBOL will permit

> ADD 7 TO DAYS.

but it will reject

> ADD "7" TO DAYS.

Punctuation

COBOL recognises three punctuation symbols: the comma, the semicolon, and the period. The comma and semicolon are optional symbols and are used only to help make the program more comprehensible.

The period is compulsory under the following conditions:

(a) immediately following Division, Section, and Paragraph names. For example

> IDENTIFICATION DIVISION.

(b) at the end of a sentence and at the end of a paragraph.

A period is not normally compulsory at the end of a Procedure

Division statement unless that statement is the last one in a paragraph. However, there are circumstances where the placing of a period after a condition test will have a major effect on the logic of the program. This will be explained in Chapter 9 when we look at condition testing.

One final rule governing the use of punctuation marks follows a conventional rule of written English. There must not be a blank character position immediately to the left of the punctuation mark. The following statement would therefore produce an error message:

MOVE 7 TO DAYS-IN-WEEK .

The punctuation mark must be followed by at least one blank character. The following line would be invalid.

MOVE 7 TO DAYS-IN-WEEK.MOVE 4 TO WEEKS-IN-MONTH.

COBOL coding form

COBOL source programs are written onto coding forms prior to entry into the computer. An example is shown in Fig. 3.5.

There are four areas on the form:
(a) Columns 1–6 are used to hold a six-digit sequence number which is used to identify each line of code. The use of sequence numbers is not compulsory but is strongly recommended. Ideally gaps should be left between line numbers so that lines may be inserted if required. For example, lines may be sequenced with gaps of 100 such as

000100
000200
000300

(b) Column 7 is the Indicator Area which denotes the use of the line. This may contain one of

(i) a blank character, which is the normal condition.
(ii) a hyphen, used to indicate a continuation line, where the preceding line was unable to hold the whole of a non-numeric literal. The use of continuation lines is explained below.
(iii) an asterisk, used to denote that the entire line contains comments. The comments are simply listed and do not form part of the compiled program. It is generally recommended that comment lines are inserted into the text to help explain what the program is meant to be doing.

29

CODING FORM

PAGE........OF........

TITLE: PROGRAMMER: DATE:

```
020000  DATA DIVISION.
020100  FD  OUT-FILE.
020200  01  OUT-REC      PIC X(60).
020300  WORKING-STORAGE SECTION.
020400  01  HEAD-1       PIC X(60) VALUE "00000 THIS IS AN EXAMPLE OF A L
020500                   INE WHICH OVERFLOWS".
```

Fig. 3.5 A COBOL coding form

(iv) an oblique (/), which acts as a comments line as in (iii) above, but on the program listing there is a throw to the top of the next page immediately prior to the '/' comments line.

(v) a 'D', which denotes that the line is a debugging line. (See Chapter 13.)

(c) Columns 8–11 are called Area A. Division, section and paragraph names must start in Area A and are followed by a period and a space. File description and record description entries also start in Area A and are also followed by a period and a space.

(d) Columns 12–72 are known as Area B. This area contains the normal COBOL source statements.

Continuation lines

As previously mentioned, non-numeric literals are actual or 'literal' values which might be up to 128 characters in length and are bounded by quotation marks. Area B of the COBOL coding form is large enough to accommodate just 61 characters. Thus any non-numeric literal longer than 59 characters cannot be fully accommodated on one line and must be continued on the following line.

To achieve this, the first part of the literal starts in Area B and is written until column 72 is filled. On the following line a hyphen is put into column 7; a quotation mark is the next character written (in column 12 or later in Area B) to indicate the start of the continuation of the literal. (See the example in Fig. 3.5.)

Summary

The chapter has examined the overall structure of a COBOL program as a series of instructions compartmentalised in Divisions. These Divisions define the operating environment of the program and its files, define the files and other data areas, and then define the procedures which manipulate the previously defined data. The rules governing the construction of words acceptable to COBOL have also been explained. These words may be reserved words, having specific meanings, or programmer-defined words. The chapter ended with a look at the formal entry of COBOL source program lines on coding forms.

Self-test questions

1 The following COBOL instructions contain a mixture of reserved words and programmer-defined words. Indicate the types of words used in each case.
   (a) ADD 1 TO LINE-COUNT.
   (b) DIVIDE TOTAL-VALUE BY TOTAL-QUANTITY
       GIVING AVERAGE.
   (c) DATA DIVISION.
   (d) MOVE SPACES TO PRINT-LINE.

2 What is the error in each of the following lines?
   (a) ADD -SUB TO TOTAL.
   (b) WORKING STORAGE SECTION.
   (c) ADD 1. TO LINE-TOTAL.
   (d) MOVE "THE CROWD SHOUTED "HURRAY" " TO
       PRINT-LINE.
   (e) SUBTRACT "7" FROM DAYS.

3 List the four Divisions in the correct sequence.

4 Where is the period (.) used?

4
COBOL data file structure

COBOL permits data to be stored as files, that is as collections of similar records, on magnetic disc. Data may also be output as print files. To help understand the nature of data files we might take as a typical example of a COBOL program the processing of customers' orders.

The normal procedure might be for a clerk to take handwritten orders, including those originating by telephone, and enter them into the computer system. But precisely what needs to be entered? The essential detail of the order relates to the customer, the product or products required and the quantity or quantities, together with backup reference information such as date of order, order number, etc. This bare information can be processed to produce an invoice/ delivery note and, subsequently, statements; it can also be used to produce analyses of sales by product, or by date, or by customer, etc.

For each order received the clerk could enter the customer's name and address, the full description of each product and its price. But this would be quite unnecessary in a properly designed computer system. The computer could have stored on disc a customer file which contains a reference number as an identifying record key, together with name, address and any other required detail. On receiving an entered customer number, the computer can be programmed to access the customer file and retrieve the appropriate record. Similarly, the computer program could have access to a products file consisting of an identifying record key (the product code), together with description, price, etc. Files such as the customer file and the product file might be termed 'reference files' because the basic requirement of the computer system is to make reference to individual records in those files in random order.

The actual transaction will be stored on file in a different manner because the processing requirements are different. Thus for each product ordered by each customer we might create a record consisting of

order number
order date

33

customer number
product code
quantity

This file could subsequently be sorted to customer sequence for any further processing that is customer oriented (such as invoices and statements), and to product code sequence for production oriented processing (such as sales analysis).

The way in which a file will be structured will thus depend upon a number of factors:

(a) whether there is a need to retrieve randomly particular records very quickly. Reference files such as product files and customer files may well have such a requirement.

(b) whether the data is transactions data which may need to be sorted to different sequences for different purposes.

(c) whether there is a need to access and process the data stored on a disc file both sequentially and randomly. For example, the records on the product file may need to be accessed randomly when processing customers' orders. But the product file may also need to be available in product number sequence in order that price lists be printed.

(d) the structure of the 'key' to the record.

COBOL allows for three methods of organizing files: sequential; indexed; and relative.

Sequential files

A sequential file is one in which the records are physically stored on disc in the sequence in which they are written. Once written, the records are retrieved and processed in the same sequence. In order to access any particular record the program would have to read all the preceding records from the beginning of the file. Each record occupies the number of characters as specified in the record description (see next chapter); the advantage of this method is that it is economic in its use of disc storage.

The sequential file can be easily extended to allow for the insertion of new records at the end of the file. Records cannot be readily deleted from a sequential file. The deletion of records requires that the data records on the file be copied to an output file; the deletion process simply consists of not copying the record to be deleted onto the output file.

34

An example of where sequential file organisation would be used is where transactions data is entered into the system in no particular key sequence and may be sorted later on; for example customer orders, which may be entered into the system in the sequence in which they were received by the company.

Indexed files

Indexed file organisation provides the facility to access and process stored records either sequentially or randomly. Indeed, during processing it is possible to switch from random to sequential processing and back again at will.

The indexed file is, in fact, a pair of files:

(a) the data file, in which the data records are stored in the physical sequence in which they were written. It thus has all the characteristics of a sequential file.
(b) the index file. This contains the keys of all the stored records together with pointers which relate the keys to the position on the data file where the corresponding data record is stored.

The major processing feature of an indexed file is the use of a record key to distinguish one record from another. A record key is the unique identifying field contained within the record. For example, the record key of a customer file would be the customer number, each customer having a unique number.

To create a new customer record, a customer record with a new customer number is written to the file. COBOL will not allow duplicate record keys. That is, it will not permit two or more different records to have the same record key contents. The data record is physically written in the next available position on the disc; the index file has a new record written to it consisting of the new key and a pointer to indicate where the corresponding record is stored.

To retrieve the record sequentially, the file is processed as though it were a sequential file, without any need to refer to the record key. COBOL presents the records to the program in ascending key sequence. It should be noted that if there are many data records stored on the file, and the data is not itself stored in key sequence, processing times can be lengthy. This is because although the program need not refer to the record key, the run-time system will use the index to ensure that data records are processed in key sequence. This may lead to a great deal of searching for the records.

To retrieve records randomly, the program is so written that the program specifies the record key to be accessed. If the corresponding record does not exist, this is regarded as an error condition and the program must have some instructions to cope with the eventuality.

Records may be deleted from indexed files. The delete instruction does not physically remove the deleted record from the disc; it merely tags the record as unavailable for further access.

To summarise, indexed organization provides the user with the best of both worlds in that data may be stored and retrieved sequentially and/or randomly. But a price has to be paid for the facility. This price is the extra disc space required for the index file, and the possibility of slow processing if the data is not itself stored in record key sequence.

It is possible to overcome the problem of slow processing by the occasional reorganization of the data file. For example, it is possible to write a program which will read the indexed file sequentially and write the data records to a sequential file, and then rewrite the data to the indexed file format. But again, such procedures take time.

Indexed file organization is common for reference files such as customer name and address files, where the records may sometimes be accessed sequentially and sometimes randomly.

Relative files

A relative file is one in which the records are stored in specific positions relative to the beginning of the file. The record key is used to indicate directly or indirectly the relative record position (or relative key, as it is called).

If the files uses a simple sequence code as the record key, then the record key may be used directly to set up the relative key. For example, if the customers on a customer file are encoded simply as 1, 2, 3, . . . 1000, the file may be created as a relative file as follows. Before writing the record to the disc, the contents of the record key is moved to a relative key field, which is described in the WORKING-STORAGE SECTION. This is to ensure that the data record is stored in its correct position relative to the start of the file.

It is worth noting that there is no need to create the file records in any particular sequence—the system will automatically store the records in their correct sequence. Records may then be retrieved sequentially without referring to the relative key; they can be retrieved randomly very quickly by using the relative key to indicate the position of the stored record.

Such a method of file organisation will provide the fastest possible random retrieval of data records stored on a disc file. However, in

36

practice, files which use simple sequence codes as their record keys often have large gaps between the keys. For example, customers may be numbered 1, 2, 4, 11, 19, 20, 47, . . . In this case there would be physical gaps on the disc file; the gaps represent wasted space because no data is stored in the relative record positions corresponding to the missing keys. Random processing will still be as fast as in the case where there are no gaps, but sequential processing will be somewhat slower because the disc reading mechanism must still pass over the unoccupied areas of the relative file.

As a general rule, provided there are not too many large gaps between the record keys, the file which has a simple sequence code as the record key is better stored in the form of a relative file than as an indexed file.

Of course, not all files are constructed in so simple a manner. The record keys may show large gaps or may contain alphabetic characters. To use relative file organization for these more difficult cases necessitates the use of a key transformation formula.

The formula should:

(a) be so designed that it can reduce any record key to a number which can be used as the relative key;
(b) have some way of dealing with alphabetic codes, if they are used in the record key, by converting them into some numeric equivalent;
(c) be able to minimise the number of record position of storage on disc; and
(d) minimise the number of duplicate relative keys.

Key transformation methods

The method used to convert a record key into a relative key will depend upon the construction of the record key and the maximum number of disc storage positions to be used. The requirement is to convert the record key into a relative record position from 1 to n, where n is the number of records in the file. Some examples follow.

The simplest case is where the record key is a sequence code starting at a value higher than 1. Thus if the first record key is 1000, the key can be transformed by deducting 999 from the record key to give the relative key as follows:

Record key	Relative key
1000	1
1001	2
1002	3
.	.
.	.
.	4
2500	1501

Another simple example is where the record key consists of say one alphabetic character and two numbers, such as A25 or X47. The letters A . . . Z are converted to their numeric equivalent 1 . . . 26, and then 1 is deducted from this numeric equivalent.

Thus the relative key is in two parts: the first part contains the value 00–25 (reflecting the alphabetic part of the record key), and the second part the numeric portion of the record key. In such a case the conversion gives the following results.

Record key	Relative key
A01	0001
.	.
A99	0099
B01	0101
.	.
B99	0199
.	.
Z01	2501
Z99	2599

A more complex example is where there are large gaps of varying sizes between record keys. One approach is to use prime number division.

Suppose there are 1000 records to be stored. The record key is divided by the nearest prime number below the number of records (in this case 997). The quotient is discarded; the remainder plus 1 is used as the relative record position. The reason for using remainder plus 1 is that the remainder may be zero and we cannot have a relative record position of zero. For example, a record with the record key of 1320 would be stored in relative record position 324, because the formula gives

$$\frac{1320}{997} = 1, \text{ remainder } 323 \ (+1) = 324$$

The main snag in using this method is that there could be some duplication of relative keys. Dividing by 997 would give a relative record position of 324 to records with the keys 323, 1320, 2317, 4311, 5308, and so on.

When the records are created, the program would have to include tests for duplicates and store them in the next available position at the end of the data file. Similarly, when accessing records, the record stored in the calculated record position may not be the required data record, in which case there would be a need to search for the required record in the overflow are at the end of the file.

Another approach, which may sometimes give a more even spread is 'square, enfold and extract'. As before, suppose there are 1000 records to be stored. The record key is squared. The digits at the front half are added to the digits at the back half, and the relative key would be extracted from the sum of the two halves.

For example, if the record key is 1320, the procedure would be:

(i) $1320^2 = 01742400$
(ii) The result is split into two halves, the front half being 0174 and the back half 2400
(iii) Add the two halves
        $0174 + 2400 = 2574$
(iv) Extract the value 257
(v)   The relative key would be $257 + 1 = 258$

It would obviously require some experimentation to find the key transformation algorithm which produces the fewest duplicates.

Choice of file organization method

The decision as to which file organisation method to adopt for a particular file is not always critical in mainframe computer systems. This is because mainframe computers tend to be so fast that relative inefficiency may be masked. Furthermore, data transfer will be slowed by frequent disc drive arm movements in a multiprogramming system. But on a microcomputer system, where only one program may be running at any one time, any inefficiency in file organization could lead to a noticeable degradation in the processing performance.

As mentioned at the start of the chapter, the method chosen will normally depend upon:

(a) the structure of the record key;
(b) whether particular records need to be accessed very quickly;
(c) whether the file is always processed sequentially or randomly;
(d) whether the data records need to be sorted into some other sequence for further processing.

For fastest processing of reference files, such as customer account files, which may need to be accessed sequentially in some programs and randomly in others, relative file organization should be chosen if at all possible. But it does require that the record key is easily converted to a relative record position. If the record key is large or complex, then indexed file organization makes for easier programming, but at a price of possibly substantially slower processing—especially if the file is composed of many hundreds of records.

If the data stored on the file is always to be retrieved sequentially, or if it is composed of transactions data which required subsequent sorting before matching against reference files, then sequential organisation is generally recommended.

Because access to records tends to be much slower if floppy discs are used, it may under some circumstances be worth considering yet another possibility—holding a reference file as a table in the program itself. This method might be adopted if:

(a) the file consists of a number of records few enough to be accommodated permanently in the Working-Storage Section of the program; and
(b) the file is stable, that is it is not subject to frequent change, which would require program changes and subsequent recompilation of the source program.

Summary

This chapter has examined the three methods of disc file organization available to COBOL users, indicating the advantages and limitations of each. Because of the relatively slow disc processing speed the choice of file organization method may be critical. It is generally recommended that indexed files be used for fairly small files and relative organization where the record key is easily converted to a relative record position. It introduced another option, namely holding reference files as tables in the program.

Self-test questions

1 What is meant by a relative file?

2 How is an indexed file structured?

3 Is is possible to retrieve records stored on a sequential file randomly?

4 What is the problem of duplicates and how can it be minimised?

5

Data file selection and description

File selection

In COBOL a file is a collection of similar records, such as customers, products, and so on. The first reference to every file used in the program is made in the FILE-CONTROL paragraph of the INPUT-OUTPUT section of the ENVIRONMENT DIVISION. The program provides the following information about the files:

(a) the name by which the file will be referred to elsewhere in the program;
(b) the name of the file as known to the operating system (CP/M) and the disc drive reference number;
(c) the method of file organization, that is whether the file is of sequential, indexed or relative type of organization;
(d) the method of file access, that is whether data records are to be accessed sequentially, in random order, or in some combination of the two; and
(e) information about the key.

For example, the coding might read as follows:

```
ENVIRONMENT DIVISION
        .
        .
        .
INPUT-OUTPUT SECTION.
FILE-CONTROL.
    SELECT PRODUCT-FILE
        ASSIGN TO "PRODUCT.DAT"
        ORGANIZATION IS INDEXED
        ACCESS IS SEQUENTIAL
        RECORD KEY IS PRODUCT-NO.
```

The entry above tells the compiler that the program will make reference to a file by the name PRODUCT-FILE. In the program all references to the file will quote the name PRODUCT-FILE. Further, when the program is run, the required file will be found on the disc mounted on the first disc drive (drive A), and the file is catalogued in the CP/M disc index as PRODUCT.DAT.

The data file is organised in an indexed form and the records are to be accessed in ascending key sequence. The control of the sequencing is through the record key, which is a field (or data element) contained within the record. This key is described later, in the Data Division of the program, with the name PRODUCT-NO. Note the use of quotation marks in the ASSIGN clause, the external file name being a non-numeric literal value.

The program element for file selection:

> SELECT internal-file-name ASSIGN TO external-file--identifier

is common to all files in the COBOL program.

Normally the external file identifier is explicit such as 'PRODUCT.DAT' or 'B.CUSTNAME.DAT'. However, the program may be so written that any one of several existing disc files can be processed, the decision as to which being left until the computer operator starts to run the program.

In this case the entry may read

> SELECT CUSTNAME-FILE ASSIGN TO FILE-NAME
> ORGANIZATION . . .
>   ACCESS . . .

where FILE-NAME is an entry of the Working-Storage Section. Before the file is opened for processing, the program would have to give the operator the opportunity to tell the program which file, stored on which disc drive, was to be selected for processing.

For example, the entry may read

> SELECT BUDGET-FILE ASSIGN TO BUDG-FNO
>   ORGANIZATION RELATIVE ACCESS SEQUENTIAL
>   RELATIVE KEY REL-KEY

The entry BUDG-FNO would need to have the actual name of the data file moved to it through an instruction in the Procedure Division such as

> MOVE "B:1984BUDG.DAT" to BUDG-FNO.

The ORGANIZATION statement refers to the method of organization of the data file. Thus an indexed file would require the statement

> ORGANIZATION IS INDEXED

a relative file would require

ORGANIZATION IS RELATIVE

and a sequential file

ORGANIZATION IS SEQUENTIAL.

The ACCESS statement is required only by indexed and relative files; records stored on sequential files can be processed sequentially only.

Indexed and relative files allow for three access methods:

(a) sequential, where records are accessed in ascending key sequence;

(b) random, where the sequence of access is controlled by the key selection in the program. In the case of an indexed file the required key is put into the field specified in the RECORD KEY clause prior to access; for a relative file the relative record position of the required record is put into the field specified in the RELATIVE KEY clause prior to access; and

(c) dynamic, where the program may switch from random access to sequential access and vice versa during the execution of the program.

Print files

Print files are selected in a similar way to disc-based files but without reference to the disc specific elements. The term used by CIS COBOL to refer to the printer is :LP:.

Thus the selection statement might read

SELECT PRINT-FILE ASSIGN TO ":LP:".

Again, note the way the external file is referenced with the use of quotation marks.

File description

For each file selected in the ENVIRONMENT DIVISION there will be a file description (FD) entry which represents the highest level of organization in the FILE SECTION of the DATA DIVISION. The format of the file description is normally

FD filename.

The file name must be identical to that in the file selection entry. So we might use the coding

SELECT PRODUCT-FILE ASSIGN TO "PRODUCT.DAT"

. . .

. . .

DATA DIVISION.
FILE SECTION
FD PRODUCT-FILE.

Mainframe versions of COBOL use various clauses as part of the FD entry to indicate particular features of the file being described. These clauses are generally not required in microcomputer versions of COBOL. However, for sake of completeness these will be listed and explained briefly. The entry may read

FD   PRODUCT-FILE
     BLOCK CONTAINS 1 RECORD
     RECORD CONTAINS 41 CHARACTERS
     LABEL RECORDS ARE OMITTED
     DATA RECORD IS PRODUCT-RECORD.

The clauses are really self-explanatory. The BLOCK clause denotes the number of records (or characters in some cases) to the block, the block being the unit of data actually transferred between the computer and the input-output device at any one time. In practice, as far as COBOL programs in microcomputer systems are concerned, the block and the record are effectively one and the same thing, despite the fact that CP/M uses a fixed block size of 128 characters on disc files. The run-time system controls the blocking on writing and deblocking on reading of data records.

RECORD CONTAINS indicates the number of characters in the record. In practice, the size of the record is implied from the sum of the sizes of the constituent data items. The clause is therefore superfluous even in mainframe versions of COBOL.

The LABEL RECORDS clause is used in mainframe systems to indicate whether the data file has standard header and/or trailer record labels associated with it. CP/M disc files are internally controlled and therefore the clause is not used.

DATA RECORD tells the compiler the name of the record associated with the file. In practice, this is not required as the name of the 01 entry is assumed to be the name of the record.

Record description

Data records are described in a hierarchical manner, using a system of level numbers to denote the position of the data item in the hierarchy.

A record will be defined as a level 01 entry. The record is composed of fields, each of which is defined as a level 02 entry. A field may itself be subdivided into sub-fields, each sub-field being defined as a level 03 entry (see Fig. 5.1). A sub-field may be further subdivided, and so on. COBOL permits up to 49 levels of hierarchical data entry.

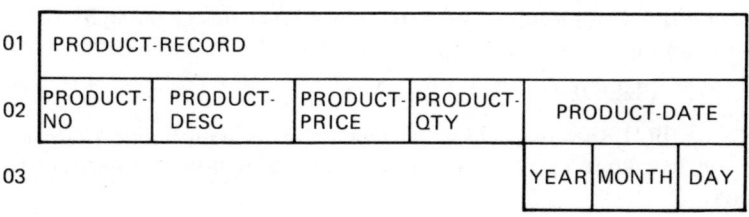

Fig. 5.1 A data record

It is necessary for the system to be informed of the size of the record:

(a) so that adequate space in memory storage can be allocated to hold the record; and
(b) in order to ensure that disc file operations are correctly handled by the run-time system.

COBOL uses an implicit method of indicating the size of the record. The record is composed of a series of successive fields, defined at level 02. The record is said to be a group item, and its fields are elementary items.

The size of the elementary item is always stated; the size of the group item is the sum of the sizes of the constituent elementary items. For example:

```
FD    PRODUCT-FILE.
01    PRODUCT-RECORD.
      02    PRODUCT-NO        PIC X(5).
      02    PRODUCT-DESC      PIC X(20).
      02    PRODUCT-PRICE     PIC 9(4)V99.
      02    PRODUCT-QTY       PIC 9(4).
      02    PRODUCT-DATE.
            03    PRODUCT-YEAR      PIC 99.
            03    PRODUCT-MONTH     PIC 99.
            03    PRODUCT-DAY       PIC 99.
```

45

In this example, PRODUCT-RECORD is a group item composed of five fields. One of the fields, PRODUCT-DATE, is itself a group item containing elementary sub-fields. The other fields are elementary items.

COBOL uses the PICTURE (or PIC, which is an acceptable abbreviation) clause to describe the general characteristics of the elementary item. The PICTURE clause gives extensive capabilities to data handling and manipulation, as will be seen later. The general format of the clause is a string of characters, each of which tells COBOL something about the characteristics of the field.
For example

    02   PRODUCT-NO   PIC X(5).

tells COBOL that the field is five characters in length, and that each of the five characters may contain any valid alphanumeric character.

    02   PRODUCT-QTY   PIC 9(4).

indicates that the field is four characters in length, and each position must contain a numeral.

But not all numeric fields are composed of whole numbers (integers). COBOL permits the use of an assumed or implied decimal point, denoted by the PICTURE element 'V'. Thus

    02   PRODUCT-PRICE   PIC 9(4)V99.

tells COBOL that the field is six characters long, four of which are to the left of the decimal point, the other two to the right.

A field described as PIC A would be assumed to contain an alphabetic character or a space.

Returning to the example given above, the field PRODUCT-DATE has an implied size of six characters, taken from the sum of the sizes of its sub-fields; while the record, PRODUCT-RECORD, has an implied size of 41 characters.

Most commonly, the programmer makes up data names as required. There is, however, one special name—FILLER. FILLER indicates to the compiler that space has to be set aside for data storage, but that those particular storage positions will not be directly referenced. The rules pertaining to PICTURE clauses apply as much to FILLER entries as to any other, though most commonly FILLER data items are described by means of PICTURE X entries.

Summary

This chapter has looked at the programming requirements for the processing of data files. It examined the relationship between files and records on the one hand, and records and fields on the other. The notion of a hierarchical structure of data descripion was introduced, together with the use of the PICTURE clause as a means of defining both size and class of a data item.

Selt-test questions

1 What is meant by

(a) the ORGANIZATION clause, and
(b) the ACCESS clause in the SELECT statement?

2 What, if anything, is wrong with the following coding

```
SELECT IN-FILE ASSIGN "B:INDATA"
     ORGANIZATION SEQUENTIAL.
     .
     .
FD   INFILE.
01   INREC.
     02   .
     02   .
```

3 How many levels of hierarchical data entry are permitted?

4 A record is described as

```
01   PERSONNEL-RECORD.
     02   PERS-NO            PIC 9(4).
     02   PERS-NAME          PIC X(20).
     02   PERS-BIRTHDATE.
          03   PERS-BDAY     PIC 99.
          03   PERS-BMONTH   PIC 99.
          03   PERS-BYEAR    PIC 99.
     02   PERS-STARTDATE.
          03   PERS-SDAY     PIC 99.
          03   PERS-SMONTH   PIC 99.
          03   PERS-SYEAR    PIC 99.
     02   PERS-DEPT          PIC XX.
```

(a) what is the length of the record?
(b) list the group items.

6
Working-Storage data

Data stored in WORKING-STORAGE is defined in the same way as in the FILE SECTION. Group items are subject to the same rules governing hierarchy. Elementary non-contiguous items, that is successive items which are not directly associated with one another, may be defined at level 01 or at a special level 77.
Thus the entries

    01   SURNAME   PIC X(30).
    77   SURNAME   PIC X(30).

are equally acceptable.

Note that some COBOL compilers require 77 entries to be entered at the start of the Working-Storage Section.

The USAGE clause

The amount of storage space occupied by a field is determined by the PICTURE clause. The entry

    01   SURNAME   PIC X(30).

will cause 30 characters to be allocated to the field 'SURNAME'. This type of entry is said to be of USAGE type 'DISPLAY' and is the most common type of data usage.

There are some exceptions to the rule of one data storage character per PICTURE element, and these exceptions govern some numeric, that is PIC 9, entries. These are:

(a) *Signed numeric fields*
The description

    02   PRODUCT-QTY   PIC 9(4)

will give an unsigned field four characters in length whose value can range from 0 to 9999.
The description

02   PRODUCT-QTY   PIC S9(4)

will give a field four characters in length with the sign contained within the final (trailing) character.

The field may be described as having the sign set in some explicit position at the start or end within the field or as a separate character. For example

02   PRODUCT-QTY   PIC S9(4) SIGN IS LEADING.

will give a four-character field with the sign set in the first (leading) character, whereas

02   PRODUCT-QTY   PIC S9(4) SIGN IS LEADING SEPARATE CHARACTER.

will give a five-character field, the first being the sign, and the following four characters the numeric data.

Similarly.

02   PRODUCT-QTY   PIC S9(4) SIGN IS TRAILING SEPARATE CHARACTER.

will give a five-character field, but this time the sign is the final character.

In all cases where a separate character is specified for the sign, the sign character will contain + or −.

(b) Numeric fields stored in binary form

In the previous case each numeral occupied one eight-bit byte or character of memory storage. It is possible to reduce storage requirements by holding data in pure binary form by means of the USAGE IS COMP clause (or USAGE IS COMPUTATIONAL).

The actual number of bytes of storage required will depend upon the number of 9s in the PICTURE clause and on whether the field is signed. In general, the number of bytes required is about half the number of characters in the field. Thus

02   THIS-VAL PIC 9(6) USAGE COMP.

will cause three bytes of storage to be set aside.

(c) *Numeric data stored in packed decimal form*

This, too, provides economy of storage of numeric data. The general idea is that the eight-bit byte can be divided into two four-bit half-bytes, each one of which can store the binary equivalent of one decimal numeral. Thus a single byte may hold two binary coded decimal numerals. The sign is stored in the trailing half-byte.

To use the packed decimal format requires the USAGE IS COMP-3 clause (or USAGE IS COMPUTATIONAL-3). For example

02   STOCK-IN-HAND   PIC S9(6) USAGE COMP-3

If a PICTURE field is described as COMP or COMP-3, then the PICTURE must be defined as numeric. That is, it may contain 9s, the operational sign 'S', the assumed decimal point 'V', and one or more of the assumed decimal scaling character 'P'. The use of decimal points and assumed decimal scaling characters will be considered in more detail below when the PICTURE clause elements are considered further.

The word USAGE, by the way, is optional. Thus

02   STOCK-IN-HAND   PIC 9(6) COMP-3.

is quite adequate for telling the compiler that the field is a numeric data item stored in packed binary coded decimal format.

While it is more common to define the USAGE of elementary data fields (i.e. normally level 02 and lower), it is permissible to define the USAGE at group level (i.e. at level 01). However, if the USAGE is defined at group level, it will apply to all the elementary items that constitute the group. Thus the definition

```
01   SALES-DETAILS   USAGE COMP-3.
     02   PRODUCT-CODE   PIC9(4).
     02   DESCRIPTION    PIC X(20).
     02   LAST-MONTH     PIC 9(6).
     02   THIS-MONTH     PIC 9(6).
```

would be illegal, as one field, DESCRIPTION, is of incompatible USAGE.

Data alignment

Of no small significance are the data alignment rules. For example if the program is required to read names and addresses from a customer file and to print those names and addresses on a document going out to the customers, it is common to have each line left-justified, as in

JA SMITH & CO.
117 LINCOLN ROAD
READING

This means that the print data field must receive the data left-justified.

Similarly, with numeric data fields there is a need to align data on the decimal point. For example, suppose a data field, PRICE, contains the price to be charged per item. The data item definition may be

02   PRICE   PIC 9(4)V99

This means that the data item definition is constructed as shown in Fig. 6.1; that is, as a six-digit data field with an assumed (not an actual) decimal point, the first four digits containing pounds and the last two digits pence. If the price were £12.00, it would be stored as 001200.

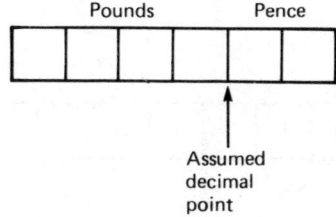

Fig. 6.1 Construction of a numeric data item definition

The rules for data alignment depend upon the category of the receiving data item. The rules are:

(a) If the receiving field is defined as alphabetic or alphanumeric, the data is sent aligned left. Any surplus receiving characters are filled with spaces; if the receiving field is shorter than the sending field truncation takes place on the right-hand end. For example

02   NAME-1   PIC X(10).

02   RECEIVE-1   PIC X(8).
02   RECEIVE-2   PIC X(12).
         .

MOVE NAME-1 TO RECEIVE-1 RECEIVE-2.

This is illustrated in Fig. 6.2.
(b) If the receiving field is numeric, the data is aligned first on assumed decimal point (if any), and the data is moved to left and right, truncating or zero-filling as required. For example

02   VAL-1   PIC 99V99.
02   VAL-2   PIC 9(4).
02   VAL-3   PIC 99.
02   VAL-4   PIC 9V9.
02   VAL-5   PIC V999.
         .

MOVE VAL-1 TO VAL-2 VAL-3 VAL-4 VAL-5.

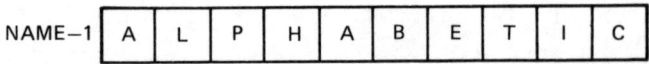

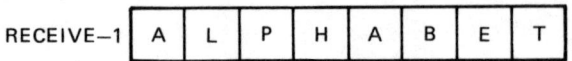

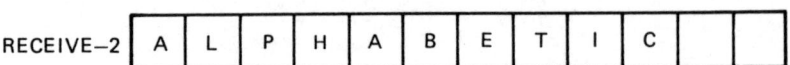

Fig. 6.2

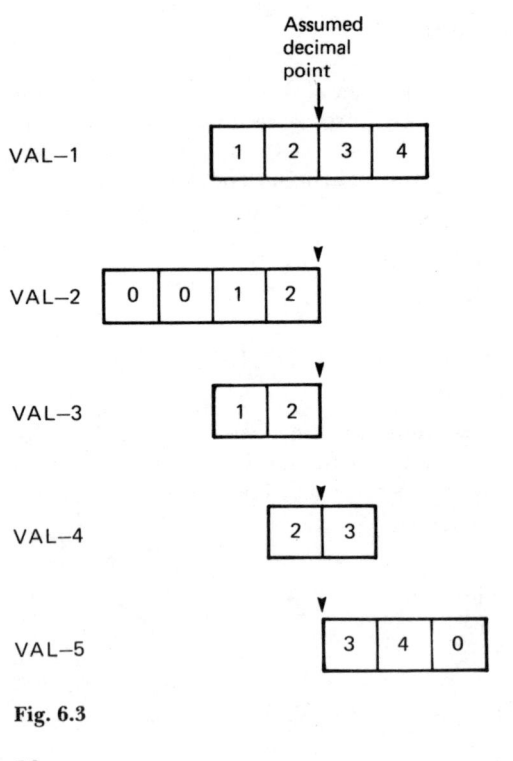

Fig. 6.3

The effects will be as shown in Fig. 6.3.

(c) If the receiving field is numeric edited, the data is again aligned first on decimal point with data movement left and right. But leading zeros may be replaced. (Editing is explained in detail in Chapter 8.)

However, the rules concerning alignment of alphabetic data may be overruled by the JUSTIFIED clause. For example

    02   NAME-1   PIC X(10).

    02   RECEIVE-1   PIC X(8) JUSTIFIED.
    02   RECEIVE-2   PIC X(12) JUSTIFIED.

    MOVE NAME-1 TO RECEIVE-1 RECEIVE-2.

will have the effects shown in Fig. 6.4. Note that this time the truncation and space fill take place on the left-hand end.

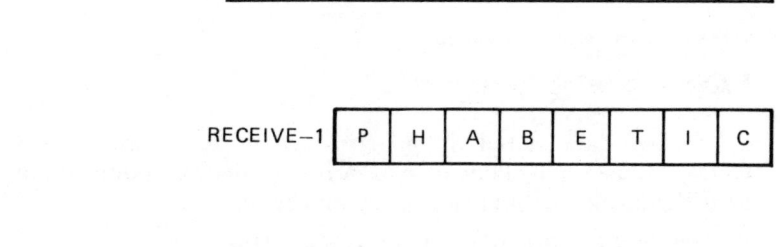

Fig. 6.4

For data stored in binary format (USAGE IS COMP), up to eight bytes are required to hold a data item (of up to 18 decimal digit equivalent). The actual number of bytes required will depend upon the number of PICTURE '9' characters and whether the data field contains a sign. For example

    02   VAL   PIC 9(6)   USAGE COMP.

will cause a three-byte field to be defined. A value of, say, 1246 would be held as shown in Fig. 6.5.

If the data field is defined as signed, then the data is stored in twos-complement form. This works as follows. When the value is positive the leftmost (most significant) bit position is set to 0; when

Byte   1   2   3

00000000	00000100	11100000

Fig. 6.5

the value is negative, the leftmost bit position is set to 1 and the binary complement is formed by inverting every 1 and 0 after the least significant bit. The process is illustrated in Fig. 6.6.

000000000000001010

shows a field described as

     PIC S9(3) USAGE COMP value + 10

111111111111110110

shows the same field, but value—10

Fig. 6.6 The twos complement form

Numeric data stored in binary coded decimal form (USAGE COMP-3) uses half of one byte to store each decimal numeral plus a least significant half-byte for the sign. The result of

     02   VAL   PIC 9(6)   USAGE COMP-3.

where the contents are 1246, is shown in Fig. 6.7. The F(1111) in the sign half-byte indicates a positive value and a non-printing sign.

     Byte   1   2   3

	0	1	2	4	6	F
Decimal						
Binary	0000	0001	0010	0100	0110	1111

Fig. 6.7

Data synchronization

Data alignment in some computer systems may also be governed by the SYNCHRONIZED (or SYNC) clause. This, however, is not a problem on most microcomputer systems in use. On mainframe

54

computers the SYNC clause is used to ensure that elementary data items are aligned on the natural word boundaries of memory storage. These are natural boundaries delimiting each data item. Each byte or character in the computer's memory may store one alphanumeric character of part of a binary or binary coded decimal value.

Generally speaking, in microcomputer versions of COBOL each data field occupies a certain number of whole bytes of memory storage. Thus

    02   NAME-1   PIC X(4).

indicates that a data field, NAME-1, is to be defined as being four bytes in length. If NAME-1 contains the value 'FRED', the bit pattern will be shown in Fig. 6.8.

Byte	1	2	3	4
Character	F	R	E	D
Bit pattern	01000110	01010010	01000101	01000100

Fig. 6.8

The issue of word boundaries is significant in mainframe computers where the word length may be two or four bytes. Efficient operation may sometimes demand that the whole of a data item be contained within word boundaries so that no word contains data to two separate data items.

Data definition—the PICTURE clause

As mentioned in the previous chapter, the size and other general characteristics of a data field are described by the PICTURE (or PIC) clause.

Each elementary item needs to be defined by means of a PICTURE. The size of a group item is implied by the sum of the sizes of its component parts. But remember that a group item is not described by means of a PICTURE clause.

However, note that a level 01 entry, although normally used to define a group item, may be an elementary item. For example

    01   NAME-AND-ADDRESS.
          02   NAME   PIC X(20).
          02   ADDRESS-1   PIC X(20).

```
02   ADDRESS-2   PIC X(20).
02   ADDRESS-3   PIC X(20).
```

shows the 01 level as defining a group item. The size of the group item is 80 characters, implied by the sum of the sizes of the constituent elementary fields. But

```
01   LINE-COUNT   PIC 99.
```

and

```
01   PAGE-NO        PIC 999.
```

are examples of 01 entries as elementary data items.

The number of characters used to describe a PICTURE must not exceed 30. Hence the use of the abbreviated form of the PICTURE description. For example, an elementary item 30 characters in length may be defined as

```
02   DATA-ITEM
PIC   XXXXXXXXXXXXXXXXXXXXXXXXXXXXXX
```

If the data item were longer than 30 characters, the PICTURE could not be described in that longhand way. For example, we could have an entry

```
01   SCREEN-MAP PIC X(1920).
```

The data item itself is 1920 characters in length, but the PICTURE description is only seven characters.

(a) *Numeric data*
A numeric data field may be up to a maximum of 18 decimal digits in length. The PICTURE may consist of the symbols '9' 'P' 'S' and 'V' only.

The '9' indicates a character position which contains a numeral. Thus the entry

```
02   TOTAL   PIC 9(4).
```

denotes a data field four numerals in length.

The 'P' is used to specify the location of an assumed decimal point when the assumed decimal point is not within the number which appears in the data item. For example

```
02   VAL   PIC 9(4)PP.
```

defines a data field where the value is always stored in hundreds, such as 286400 or 172500. The data item occupies four characters of storage instead of six (thus the data field will hold 2864 instead of

56
```
```

286400), and any value stored in the data field will always be multiplied by 100 before being used in arithmetic. If, for example, TOTAL is defined as 9(4)PPP and receives the value of 1234567, the value 1234 is stored in TOTAL. (The 567 part is discarded.)

Thus the use of the 'P' symbol provides an element of economy of storage. But the use of this method may prove to be false economy because of the extra processing required whenever the contents of the data item are used.

The 'S' indicates the presence of an operational sign, but is counted as one of the characters in the data item only if the

$$\text{SIGN IS} \left\{ \begin{array}{l} \text{LEADING} \\ \text{TRAILING} \end{array} \right\} \text{SEPARATE CHARACTER}$$

clause is appended to the data description.

The 'V' indicates the location of an assumed decimal point. For example

02   PRICE   PIC 9(4)V99.

specifies that there is an assumed decimal point between the fourth and fifth digits. The assumed decimal point does not occupy any memory storage.

(b) *Edited numeric data*
The PICTURE may contain the symbols listed in (a) above. Additional symbols are available for editing purposes. These are concerned with

    (i)   suppressing and replacing leading zeros ('Z' and '*')
    (ii)   currency symbol ('£', '$')
    (iii) insertion characters (',', '.', '0', 'B', and '/')
    (iv) sign printing ('+', '−', 'DB', and 'CR')

(c) *Alphabetic data*
The PICTURE string may contain only 'A' or 'B', where the 'B' refers to the insertion of a blank character.

(d) *Alphanumeric data*
The data itself may consist of any valid character and is denoted by the symbol 'X'. Thus

02   HEADING   PIC X(120).

will give a 120-character data item which may be used to hold any characters.

(e) *Edited alphanumeric data*
The PICTURE is composed of certain combinations of '9', 'A', 'X', 'B', '0', and '/'.
The rules governing editing are discussed more fully in Chapter 8.

Setting initial values

The initial value of a data item may be set by using the VALUE clause. For example

    77   LINE-COUNT   PIC 99   VALUE 70.

will set the staring value of LINE-COUNT to 70.
    The initial value must be compatible with the PICTURE clause for the data item. So, for example,

    02   INIT-VALUE   PIC S9(4)   VALUE + 1234.

is acceptable in that the PICTURE specifies a signed value, whereas

    02   INIT-VALUE   PIC 9(4)   VALUE   +1234.

would be illegal.
    Similarly

    02   VAL   PIC 9(4)   VALUE "ABCD".

would be rejected because of incompatibility of class.
    The initial value may be set for the whole of a group item—but this must be set by a figurative constant or a non-numeric literal. For example.

    01   PRINT-LINE   VALUE SPACES.
        02   CUST-NO   PIC 9(4).
        02   FILLER   PIC X(4).
        02   CUST-NAME   PIC X(20).
        02   FILLER   PIC X(4).
        02   CUST-VAL   PIC Z(6).99.

is valid.
    It should be noted that group items are classed as though they were alphanumeric, even though some of the constituent elementary data items may be of class numeric.

Redefinition of data items

The same memory storage area can be described or defined in diffe-rent ways by means of the REDEFINES clause. For example

```
01   INPUT-CODE   PIC X(4).
01   INPUT-VAL   REDEFINES INPUT-CODE PIC 9(4).
```

shows two data items sharing the same four positions of storage.

The REDEFINES clause must immediately follow the first-named data item. Thus

```
01   INPUT-CODE   PIC 9(4).
01   INPUT-VAL PIC X(4) REDEFINES INPUT-CODE.
```

is invalid because the PIC clause precedes the REDEFINES clause.

It is important to ensure that the hierarchical levels of both data items are the same. Thus

```
03   DATA-ELEMENT   PIC X.
02   DATA-1   REDEFINES   DATA-ELEMENT   PIC 9.
```

is illegal because the level numbers are not identical.

There must not be a level number lower than in the REDEFINES data item between the redefined and the redefining data description. Thus

```
02   DATA-NUM.
     03   DATA-NUM-1   PIC 9(4).
02   DATA-NAME   PIC X(20).
     03   DATA-ALPHA-1   REDEFINES   DATA-NUM-1
     PIC X(4).
```

is illegal, and would have to be rewritten as

```
02   DATA-NUM.
     03   DATA-NUM-1   PIC 9(4).
     03   DATA-ALPHA-1   REDEFINES   DATA-NUM-1
     PIC X(4).
02   DATA-NAME   PIC X(20).
```

Redefinition is not allowed at level 77. Hence

```
77   LINE-COUNT   PIC 99.
77   LINE-1   REDEFINES   LINE-COUNT   PIC ZZ.
```

is illegal.

Redefinition is not allowed at level 01 in the File Section. Though, in fact, all 01 entries for a given file are allocated the same memory storage area. In other words, there is automatic redefinition of the record area for any file in the File Section with multiple record types.

However, redefinition at level 01 is permitted in the Working-Storage Section. Where redefinition is at level 01 the sizes of the redefined and redefining areas need not be identical. For example

```
01   DATE-HEAD   PIC X(21)   VALUE
     "Enter Date ] / / [".
01   ENTER-DATE   REDEFINES   DATE-HEAD.
     02   FILLER           PIC X(12).
     02   ENTER-DAY        PIC 99.
     02   FILLER           PIC X.
     02   ENTER-MONTH      PIC 99.
     02   FILLER           PIC X.
     02   ENTER-YEAR       PIC 99.
```

shows the original (redefined) area as 21 characters in length, whereas the redefining area is only 20 characters long.

However, if the redefinition is at any other level but 01, the sizes of both data items must be identical. For example

```
02   FIRST-VALUE   PIC 9(6).
02   VALUE-X   REDEFINES   FIRST-VALUE.
     03   FIRST-PART      PIC 9.
     03   SECOND-PART     PIC 9.
     03   THIRD-PART      PIC 9(4).
```

shows an acceptable form of redefinition at level 02.

Multiple redefinitions of a data item are permitted, but each redefinition must refer to the original data item name. For example

```
02   FIRST-VALUE   PIC 9(6).
02   VALUE-X   REDEFINES   FIRST-VALUE.
     03   FIRST-PART      PIC 9.
     03   SECOND-PART     PIC 9.
     03   THIRD-PART      PIC 9(4).
02   VALUE-Y   REDEFINES   FIRST-VALUE.
     03   PART-1   PIC 99.
     03   PART-2   PIC 9.
     03   PART-3   PIC 99.
     03   PART-4   PIC 9.
```

The original data item may contain a pre-set value. For example

```
01   SEVEN-TWENTY   PIC 999   VALUE 720.
01   RED-720   REDEFINES   SEVEN-TWENTY.
     02   SEVEN      PIC 9.
     02   TWENTY     PIC 99.
```

In this example, the data item SEVEN will contain the value 7, and the data item TWENTY will contain the value 20. But note that the VALUE clause must be specified only in the original, first-named, data item.

60

OCCURS clause and tables

So far we have described data items in detail by applying a PIC-TURE to each elementary data item.

Sometimes there may be several similar data items located immediately next to one another, i.e. contiguous data items. For example, a data record stored on disc may appear as shown in Fig. 6.9. with the product code and 12 sales value entries. This may be coded somewhat laboriously as

```
01   SALES-RECORD.
     02   PRODUCT-CODE   PIC 9(4).
     02   MONTH-1        PIC 9(6).
     02   MONTH-2        PIC 9(6).
     02   MONTH-3        PIC 9(6).
                  .
                  .
                  .
     02   MONTH-11       PIC 9(6).
     02   MONTH-12       PIC 9(6).
```

PROD CODE	MONTH 1 SALES	MONTH 2 SALES	MONTH 3 SALES	MONTH 4 SALES	MONTH 5 SALES	MONTH 6 SALES	MONTH 7 SALES	MONTH 8 SALES	MONTH 9 SALES	MONTH 10 SALES	MONTH 11 SALES	MONTH 12 SALES
4	6	6	6	6	6	6	6	6	6	6	6	6

Fig. 6.9

The OCCURS clause enables the programmer to reduce the volume of source coding. The above entry may be rewritten as

```
01   SALES-RECORD.
     02   PROD-CODE   PIC 9(4).
     02   MONTH       PIC 9(6)   OCCURS 12 TIMES.
```

This tells the compiler to set aside enough memory storage to hold a table of 12 entries, each six characters long.

It would then be necessary to devise some means of processing the individual entries in the table. This is done either through subscripting or through indexing. Both methods will be explained in detail in Chapter 11. But the essential feature is that the entry has a pointer associated with it. The pointer is coded in parentheses after the table name, and may be an integer or a data name. For example

MOVE MONTH (4) TO HOLD-AREA

would cause the value stored in the fourth entry in the table called MONTH to be moved. Do note that there must be a space immediately before the opening parenthesis and immediately after the closing parenthesis.

The OCCURS clause can reference group items as well as elementary items. For example

```
02  TABLE-ENTRY   OCCURS 4.
    03  NAME   PIC X(5).
    03  VAL    PIC 9(4).
```

will cause a table to be set up as shown in Fig. 6.10.

Name		
Val	1st entry	
Name		
Val	2nd entry	
Name		
Val	3rd entry	
Name		
Val	4th entry	

Fig. 6.10

The OCCURS clause cannot be used at level 01 nor at level 77. Thus

```
01  TABLE-ENTRIES   OCCURS 10 TIMES.
```

is illegal.

The use of the OCCURS clause is often associated with the REDEFINES clause. For example it may be required to print a three-digit abbreviation of the month name. A table of month name abbreviations may be set up and processed as follows:

```
01  MONTH-ABBREV   PIC (X36) VALUE
    'JANFEBMARAPRMAYJUNJLYAUGSEPOCT-
    NOVDEC'.
01  MONTH-ABB   REDEFINES   MONTH-ABBREV.
    02  MONTH-NAME  PIC  XXX  OCCURS    12
    TIMES.
        :
```

```
01   POINTER   PIC 99.
             :
     MOVE   MONTH-NAME   (POINTER) ' TO
     PRINT-MONTH-NAME.
```

Summary

The chapter has addressed itself mainly to definition of data which is of Working-Storage, rather than File, type. However, the rules and clauses mentioned also relate to file data definition.

It has considered the various format for holding data and has emphasised the need for compatibility between the class definition and the actual data held. It has also shown how one data area can be defined in different ways, and introduced the notion of holding data in tabular form for further processing.

Self-test questions

1 Show how the value 750 would be stored in fields described as
(a) PIC 9(6).
(b) PIC 9(4)   COMP.
(c) PIC 9(4)   COMP-3.

2 A data item, NAME-1, is defined as PIC X(10) and contains the value 'FRED SMITH'. Show the contents of the following data fields resulting from a MOVE to them:
(a) FIELD-1   PIC 9(6).
(b) FIELD-2   PIC X(4).
(c) FIELD-3   PIC X(5) JUSTIFIED.
(d) FIELD-4   PIC X(11).
(e) FIELD-5   PIC X(7).

3 Explain why the following entries are invalid:
(a) 01   STUDENT-RECORD   PIC X(30).
       02   STUDENT-NO   PIC 9(4).
       02   STUDENT-NAME   PIC X(20).
       02   STUDENT-CLASS   PIC 9(4).
       02   STUDENT-AGE   PIC 99.
(b)   02   VAL-2   PIC 9(5)S.
(c) 77   DATA-2   REDEFINES   DATA-1   PIC X(4).
(d) 01   TWO-AND-THREE   REDEFINES TWENTY-THREE.
       02   TWO   PIC 9   VALUE "2".
       02   THREE   PIC 9   VALUE "3".

7

File handling procedures

File handling procedures relate to the opening and closing of files and the reading, writing and deleting of data records stored on the files.

The File-Control paragraph of the Input-Output Section of the Environment Division tells the program that a specific data file is to be accessed, and it gives that file a name by which it is identified elsewhere in the program. The file, and the structure of its constituent records, are then described in the File Section of the Data Division.

For example, the program may contain the following entries:

```
INPUT-OUTPUT SECTION.
FILE-CONTROL.
   SELECT PRODUCT-FILE
   ASSIGN TO "PRODUCT.DAT"
   ORGANIZATION IS INDEXED ACCESS MODE IS
   SEQUENTIAL
   RECORD KEY IS PRODUCT-NO.
           :
           :
DATA DIVISION.
FILE SECTION.
FD   PRODUCT-FILE.
01   PRODUCT-RECORD.
     02   PRODUCT-NO   PIC X(5).
           :
           :
```

Data file procedures in general

(a) *OPEN*
Before the data stored on a file can be accessed, the file must be opened. The Open statement takes the form

64

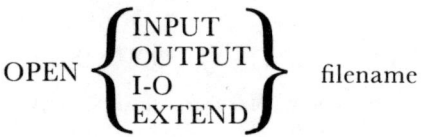

OPEN $\left\{\begin{array}{l}\text{INPUT}\\\text{OUTPUT}\\\text{I-O}\\\text{EXTEND}\end{array}\right\}$ filename

The entries INPUT, OUTPUT, I-O and EXTEND indicate whether the file is to be read from only, written to only, or may be read from and written to in the same program.

Thus the entry

OPEN INPUT PRODUCT-FILE

tells the computer that PRODUCT-FILE is to be read. Any attempt by the program to write a record to the file would result in an error condition, which would be signified by a message to the programmer when the program is compiled.

The Open statement, when executed, causes the following actions to be taken:

(i) If the file is described as INPUT, the operating system checks for the existence of the required file. Absence of the required file causes the program to halt with an error condition flagged. After opening the file, the current record pointer is set to the first record currently existing on the file. But note that the Open statement does not read the record.

(ii) If the file is described as I-O, the operating system checks for the existence of the required file. If the file does not exist, it will be created.

(iii) Opening a file described as OUTPUT causes the creation of a new file with no records, i.e. an empty file. If a file with the same name exists on the specified disc, it will be deleted and the records associated with the file will be lost.

(iv) The EXTEND option applies only to sequential disc files. It enables records to be written immediately after the last record currently stored on the file. It is thus the equivalent of the OUTPUT option, but without deleting the current records.

(b) *READ*
To read a record from a data file and make it available for processing requires the execution of the READ statement, with the file having been previously opened in the INPUT or the I-O mode.

There are two format available

(i) If the file is selected as ACCESS MODE IS SEQUENTIAL the format used is READ filename AT END imperative-statement.

For example

READ PRODUCT-FILE AT END GO TO FINISH.

Note that it is permissible to read a record into an area in Working-Storage. For example

READ PRODUCT-FILE INTO TEMP-PROD AT END . . .

where TEMP-PROD is a data area defined in the Working-Storage Section. This instruction is the equivalent of

READ PRODUCT-FILE AT END . . .
MOVE PRODUCT-RECORD TO TEMP-PROD.

and causes the data to be available in both data areas.

READ . . . AT END . . . causes the next logical record to be made available by having its contents put into the associated record area defined in the File Section of the Data Division.

If there is no next record, that is at the end of the file, the AT END path is followed and the file is not avavailable for any further reads until it is closed and then re-opened.

(ii) For files selected as ACCESS MODE IS RANDOM the format used is

READ filename INVALID KEY imperative-statement.

For example

READ PRODUCT-FILE INVALID KEY
GO TO INSERTION.

Random access to data is available only to indexed and relative files.

If the file is of organisation type indexed, the key of the required record must be put into the Record Key prior to reading the record. If a record with a matching key exists, the Read will make the record available; a mismatch will lead to the Invalid Key path being taken.

For example take the following coding:

```
FILE-CONTROL.
  SELECT PRODUCT-FILE
  ASSIGN TO "PRODUCT.DAT"
  ORGANIZATION IS INDEXED   ACCESS MODE IS
  RANDOM
    RECORD KEY IS PRODUCT-NO.
DATA DIVISION.
FILE SECTION.
FD   PRODUCT-FILE.
```

```
01   PRODUCT-RECORD.
     02   PRODUCT-NO      PIC X(5).
     02   PRODUCT-DESC    PIC X(20).
          .
          .
PROCEDURE DIVISION.
BEGIN.   OPEN INPUT PRODUCT-FILE.
          .
          .
     MOVE REQUIRED-NO TO PRODUCT-NO.
     READ PRODUCT-FILE INVALID KEY
     GO TO NOT-THERE.
```

The MOVE instruction specifies the required record. This is followed by a READ, which if unsuccessful sends control to a procedure elsewhere in the program called NOT-THERE. If the READ is successful the program continues in sequence.

For a file organised in relative mode, random access to records requires that a relative record number is put into the field described as the Relative Key prior to reading the record. If the file does not contain a record in that relative record position, then the INVALID KEY path is followed. The coding might look as follows:

```
FILE-CONTROL.
   SELECT CUSTOMER-FILE ASSIGN TO
   "B:CUST.DAT"
   ORGANIZATION IS RELATIVE ACCESS MODE IS
   RANDOM
   RELATIVE KEY IS REL-KEY.
DATA DIVISION.
FILE SECTION.
FD   CUSTOMER-FILE.
01   CUSTOMER-RECORD.
     02   CUSTOMER-NO   PIC 9(4).
          .
          .
WORKING-STORAGE SECTION.
77   REL-KEY   PIC 9(6).
          .
          .
PROCEDURE DIVISION.
BEGIN.   OPEN I-O CUSTOMER-FILE.
          .
          .
     SUBTRACT 100000 FROM WANTED-CUST GIVING
     REL-KEY.
```

READ CUSTOMER-FILE INVALID KEY
GO TO NOT-THERE.

(c) *WRITE*

The function of the WRITE statement is to write a record onto an output or input-output file. The file must be opened prior to the execution of the WRITE statement. The format for a sequential disc file is

WRITE record-name.

Indexed and relative disc files use the format

WRITE record-name INVALID KEY imperative-statement

It should be noted that COBOL requires that the WRITE statement references the record name, and not the file name. (This is in contrast with the OPEN and READ statements.)

After the record is written, the data is no longer available in the record area. However, if the write was unsuccessful as a result of an Invalid Key condition, the data will remain in the record area.

The program may specify a Write from a data area in Working-Storage. For example

WRITE OUTPUT-RECORD FROM TEMP-AREA.

which is the equivalent of

MOVE TEMP-AREA TO OUTPUT-RECORD.
WRITE OUTPUT-RECORD.

If the Write is successfully executed, the data is still available in the Working-Storage area, though not in the File area.

Indexed files are written subject to the following conditions:

(i) the Record Key must be set before executing the Write statement. This is to enable the operating system to store the record so as to enable subsequent access to it.

(ii) the value of the Record key must be unique; that is, records with duplicate keys are not permitted.

(iii) if the file was selected as ACCESS MODE SEQUEN-TIAL, the records must be presented to be written in key sequence, whereas ACCESS MODE RANDOM files may have records presented in any sequence.

Relative files are written subject to the following conditions:

(i) If ACCESS MODE SEQUENTIAL, the operating system

will set up the relative keys contents by giving the first record to be written a relative key of 1, and subsequent records relative keys of 2, 3, 4, etc.

(ii) If ACCESS MODE RANDOM, the relative key must be set before writing the record.

(iii) the relative key must not be a duplicate.

Files written directly to the printer are a special form of sequential file. The rules associated with opening and writing sequential disc files apply to printed files; but, in addition, there are rules governing line skipping and skipping to the head of form.

The WRITE statement is extended so that the format is

$$\text{WRITE record-name} \left\{ \begin{array}{l} \text{BEFORE} \\ \text{AFTER} \end{array} \right\} \text{ADVANCING} \left\{ \begin{array}{l} \text{integer-LINES} \\ \text{PAGE} \end{array} \right\}$$

An example of the way in which the use of printer files is coded is

```
INPUT-OUTPUT SECTION.
FILE-CONTROL.
   SELECT PRINT-FILE ASSIGN TO ":LP:".
DATA DIVISION.
FILE SECTION.
FD   PRINT-FILE.
01   PRINT-RECORD.
     02 . . .
     02 . . .
PROCEDURE DIVISION.
BEGIN.
   OPEN OUTPUT PRINT-FILE.
   MOVE SPACE TO PRINT-RECORD.
   WRITE   PRINT-RECORD   BEFORE   ADVANCING
   PAGE.
        :
        :
   WRITE  PRINT-RECORD  BEFORE  ADVANCING  1
   LINE.
```

The rule concerning BEFORE/AFTER ADVANCING is as follows: if BEFORE is used, the line is printed and then the paper is advanced one or more lines; if AFTER is specified, the paper is advanced prior to printing.

It is possible to overprint a line by means of the following:

```
WRITE PRINT-RECORD BEFORE ADVANCING 0 LINE.
WRITE PRINT-RECORD BEFORE ADVANCING 1 LINE.
```

(d) *CLOSE*

After processing a data file it is necessary to close it. This is done by means of the CLOSE statement in the format

CLOSE filename.

After closing a file, no statement referencing the file can be executed unless the file is re-opened. It is important to ensure that output files are closed as failure to do so can result in the loss of data records.

Programming requirements for sequential files

The essential elements of programming for sequential files is shown in the program in Fig. 7.1. This short program creates a disc file

```
000100 IDENTIFICATION DIVISION.
000200 PROGRAM-ID.    EX1.
000300 ENVIRONMENT DIVISION.
000400 CONFIGURATION SECTION.
000500 SOURCE-COMPUTER.    MODEL-XYZ.
000600 OBJECT-COMPUTER.    MODEL-XYZ.
000700 INPUT-OUTPUT SECTION.
000800 FILE-CONTROL.
000900     SELECT OUT-FILE ASSIGN TO "MONTHS.DAT"
001000         ORGANIZATION LINE SEQUENTIAL.
001100 DATA DIVISION.
001200 FILE SECTION.
001300 FD   OUT-FILE.
001400 01   OUT-REC.
001500     02   OUT-MONTH     PIC 99.
001600     02   OUT-DAYS      PIC 99.
001700     02   OUT-CUM-DAYS PIC 999.
001800 WORKING-STORAGE SECTION.
001900 01   MONTH    PIC 99   VALUE 0.
002000 01   MDAYS     PIC X(24) VALUE "312831303130313130313031".
002100 01   MDY   REDEFINES   MDAYS.
002200     02   DAYS   PIC 99   OCCURS 12.
002300 01   CUM-DAYS   PIC 999 VALUE 0.
002400*
002500 PROCEDURE DIVISION.
002600 BEGIN.
002700     OPEN OUTPUT OUT-FILE.
002800 MAIN-LOOP.
002900     ADD 1 TO MONTH.
003000     IF MONTH > 12 GO TO FINISH.
003100     MOVE MONTH TO OUT-MONTH.
003200     MOVE DAYS (MONTH) TO OUT-DAYS.
003300     ADD DAYS (MONTH) TO CUM-DAYS.
003400     MOVE CUM-DAYS TO OUT-CUM-DAYS.
003500     WRITE OUT-REC.
003600     GO TO MAIN-LOOP.
003700 FINISH.
003800     CLOSE OUT-FILE.
003900     STOP RUN.
```

Fig. 7.1

consisting of 12 records in sequence, each containing the month number, number of days in the month, and cumulative days as at the end of the month. The results are as shown in Fig. 7.2.

```
B>TYPE MONTHS.DAT
0131031
0228059
0331090
0430120
0531151
0630181
0731212
0831243
0930273
1031304
1130334
1231365
```

Fig. 7.2

The key requirements are a SELECT statement in the Environment Division, and the file handling verbs in the Procedure Division.

The first file handling instruction encountered is the OPEN and takes the form.

OPEN OUTPUT OUT-FILE.

This tells the compiler that data is to written to the file in this run. If the file specified in the SELECT does not exist it will be created. If it does exist it will be overwritten.

But suppose the program is run once to give the results as shown in Fig. 7.2, and the OPEN statement is changed to

OPEN EXTEND OUT-FILE.

and the program run again. The effect is as shown in Fig. 7.3, namely the file records are repeated. The effect of the EXTEND is to add records to the file after the end of the last existing record.

The second file handling verb used is WRITE. Note that it is the record which is written. And finally the file is CLOSED.

Input processing is treated in a similar manner. Figure 7.4 shows how the file just created is read and the output printed. The points to note here are the

OPEN INPUT M-FILE

and the

READ M-FILE AT END . . .

Also note the print file handling which is sequential output processing with the additional element of

BEFORE n LINES

```
B>TYPE MONTHS.DAT
0131031
0228059
0331090
0430120
0531151
0630181
0731212
0831243
0930273
1031304
1130334
1231365
0131031
0228059
0331090
0430120
0531151
0630181
0731212
0831243
0930273
1031304
1130334
1231365
```

Fig. 7.3

in the WRITE statement.

CIS COBOL allows for a variant of the sequential file called LINE SEQUENTIAL. The records which compose this type of file may be variable in length because the termination of the individual record is denoted by the system by means of carriage-return-line-feed characters.

This method of file organization provides sequential file compatibility with other CP/M software such as sort utilities. However, to all intents and purposes the LINE SEQUENTIAL form of organisation may be regarded as ordinary sequential and has no special programming requirements other than in the SELECT statement which may read

SELECT SEQ-FILE ASSIGN TO "TRANS.DAT"
ORGANIZATION LINE SEQUENTIAL.

Programming requirements for indexed files

Records stored on indexed files can be accessed in random order or in key sequence. The key is the constituent data item within the record which is used to determine the sequence. The record key must be unique. That is, just one record in the file may have a particular key and, in CIS COBOL, the key length must not exceed 32 characters.

72

```
000010 IDENTIFICATION DIVISION.
000020 PROGRAM-ID.    PRNT.
000030 ENVIRONMENT DIVISION.
000040 CONFIGURATION SECTION.
000050 SOURCE-COMPUTER.   MODEL-XYZ.
000060 OBJECT-COMPUTER.   MODEL-XYZ.
000070 INPUT-OUTPUT SECTION.
000080 FILE-CONTROL.
000090      SELECT M-FILE ASSIGN "MONTHS.DAT"
000100          ORGANIZATION LINE SEQUENTIAL.
000110      SELECT P-FILE ASSIGN ":LP:".
000120 DATA DIVISION.
000130 FILE SECTION.
000140 FD   M-FILE.
000150 01   M-REC.
000160      02  M-MONTH     PIC 99.
000170      02  M-DAYS      PIC 99.
000180      02  M-CUM-DAYS  PIC 999.
000190 FD   P-FILE.
000200 01   P-REC.
000210      02  FILLER     PIC XX.
000220      02  P-MONTH    PIC Z9.
000230      02  FILLER     PIC X(5).
000240      02  P-DAYS     PIC 99.
000250      02  FILLER     PIC X(6).
000260      02  P-CUM-DAYS PIC Z99.
000270      02  FILLER     PIC X(112).
000280 PROCEDURE DIVISION.
000290 BEGIN.
000300      OPEN INPUT M-FILE
000310          OUTPUT P-FILE.
000320      MOVE " MONTH   DAYS   CUM-DAYS" TO P-REC.
000330      WRITE P-REC BEFORE 2.
000340      MOVE SPACE TO P-REC.
000350 READ-FILE.
000360      READ M-FILE AT END GO TO FINISH.
000370      MOVE M-MONTH TO P-MONTH.
000380      MOVE M-DAYS TO P-DAYS.
000390      MOVE M-CUM-DAYS TO P-CUM-DAYS.
000400      WRITE P-REC BEFORE 1.
000410      GO TO READ-FILE.
000420 FINISH.
000430      CLOSE M-FILE P-FILE.
000440      STOP RUN.
```

Fig. 7.4

Figure 7.5 shows a simple program which enables data entered on the VDU screen to be written to a sequential file. During the processing there is random access to records on an indexed file, PRODUCT-FILE. The key points to note are:

(a) the form of the SELECT statement (lines 001200–001400), which provides the system with the source name, PRODUCT-FILE, the actual file name, PRODUCT.DAT, information about the ORGANIZATION and ACCESS methods, and the fact that the

```
000100 IDENTIFICATION DIVISION.
000200 PROGRAM-ID.   ORDERS1.
000300 ENVIRONMENT DIVISION.
000400 CONFIGURATION SECTION.
000500 SOURCE-COMPUTER.   MODEL-XYZ.
000600 OBJECT-COMPUTER.   MODEL-XYZ.
000700 SPECIAL-NAMES   CONSOLE IS CRT.
000800 INPUT-OUTPUT SECTION.
000900 FILE-CONTROL.
001000     SELECT ORDERS-FILE  ASSIGN TO "ORDERS.DAT"
001100         ORGANIZATION SEQUENTIAL.
001200     SELECT  PRODUCT-FILE ASSIGN TO "PRODUCT.DAT"
001300         ORGANIZATION INDEXED  ACCESS RANDOM
001400         RECORD KEY IS PRODUCT-NO.

002000 DATA DIVISION.
002100 FILE SECTION.
002200 FD  ORDERS-FILE.
002300 02  ORDERS-RECORD.
002400     02  ORDERS-CUST   PIC 9(4).
002500     02  ORDERS-PROD   PIC X(5).
002600     02  ORDERS-QTY    PIC 9(4).
002700 FD  PRODUCT-FILE.
002800 01  PRODUCT-RECORD.
002900     02  PRODUCT-NO    PIC X(5).
003000     02  FILLER        PIC X(36).

004000 WORKING-STORAGE SECTION.
004200 01  DISPLAY-SCREEN.
004300     02  FILLER   PIC X(35).
004400     02  DISP-1   PIC X(11) VALUE "ORDERS ENTRY".
004500     02  FILLER   PIC X(121).
004600     02  DISP-2   PIC X(19) VALUE "CUSTOMER NO ]     [".
004700     02  FILLER   PIC X(7).
004800     02  DISP-3   PIC X(18) VALUE "PRODUCT NO ]      [".
004900     02  FILLER   PIC X(6).
005000     02  DISP-4   PIC X(15) VALUE "QUANTITY ]      [".
005100 01  ENTER-SCREEN REDEFINES DISPLAY-SCREEN.
005200     02  FILLER   PIC X(181).
005300     02  SCREEN-CUST  PIC 9(4).
005400     02  FILLER   PIC X(20).
005500     02  SCREEN-PRODUCT  PIC X(5).
005600     02  FILLER   PIC X(17).
005700     02  SCREEN-QTY   PIC 9(4).

010000 PROCEDURE DIVISION.
010100 OPEN-FILES.
010200     OPEN INPUT PRODUCT-FILE
010300         OUTPUT ORDERS-FILE.
010400     DISPLAY SPACE.
010500     DISPLAY DISPLAY-SCREEN.
010600 INPUT-DATA.
010700     MOVE SPACE TO ENTER-SCREEN.
010800     DISPLAY ENTER-SCREEN.
010900     DISPLAY "                    " AT 1501.
011000 ENTER-INPUT.
011100     ACCEPT ENTER-SCREEN.
011200     IF SCREEN-CUST = 9999 GO TO FINISH.
011500     MOVE SCREEN-PRODUCT TO PRODUCT-NO.
011600     READ PRODUCT-FILE INVALID KEY GO TO BAD-PROD.
011700     IF SCREEN-QTY NOT NUMERIC GO TO BAD-QTY.
011800     MOVE SCREEN-CUST TO ORDERS-CUST.
011900     MOVE SCREEN-PRODUCT TO ORDERS-PROD.
012000     MOVE SCREEN-QTY TO ORDERS-QTY.
012100     WRITE ORDERS-RECORD.
012200     GO TO INPUT-DATA.
012600 BAD-PROD.
012700     DISPLAY "* INVALID PRODUCT NO *" AT 1501.
012800     GO TO ENTER-INPUT.
012900 BAD-QTY.
013000     DISPLAY "* INVALID QUANTITY *" AT 1501.
013100     GO TO ENTER-INPUT.
013200 FINISH.
013300     CLOSE ORDERS-FILE PRODUCT-FILE.
013400     STOP RUN.
```

Fig. 7.5

record key is a data item called PRODUCT-NO.

(b) the file is defined (lines 002700–003000) and the key field is explicitly defined (lines 002900).

(c) the file is initially OPENed as an INPUT file (line 002900).

(d) in order to access the file randomly, the record key is filled with the desired record number (line 011500), and the file is READ with an instruction of what to do if there is an invalid key, i.e. if the record is not found (lines 011600 and 012600–012800).

The example give above is most typical of the use of an indexed file as a reference file. The very same file can be accessed sequentially as seen in the example program at the end of Chapter 1. The main differences in approach are that the earlier program specified ACCESS IS SEQUENTIAL (line 001100), and the READ was followed by AT END (line 010500).

There is a third access mode available—DYNAMIC. In this mode records may be accessed both sequentially and randomly in the same program. This method might be used where is desired to access a master record rapidly in order to provide a starting point for further processing of subordinate records sequentially.

For example, suppose it has been estimated that processing of a sales ledger would be quicker if the customer name and address were merged with sales invoices to form a single file. As an indexed file there would have to be a single record key, and for processing purposes the name and address details would have to precede sales invoice details.

If name and address details occupy more storage space than sales invoice details it would be possible to provide greater equality in record size by creating three record types:

(a) the key, plus name and two lines of address;
(b) the key, plus two lines of address and telephone number;
(c) the key, plus sales invoice detail.

The record may look like Fig. 7.6, with the record key as a composite data item, and the File Description might look like Fig. 7.7.

When printing the end-of-month statements, the file would be accessed sequentially. The reading of a new record with a suffix of 00 would cause totals, etc for the previous customer to be printed prior to printing name and address headings for the current customer.

But for enquiries as to the current state of the customer's account and for the printing of one-off documents for a particular customer, the ACCESS MODE IS DYNAMIC clause would have to be selected. In the Procedure Division, the customer would be accessed randomly by moving the customer number to the customer part of

Record Type 1

Customer no and suffix	1–6	(suffix = 00)
Name	7–26	
Address	27–66	(2 lines @ 20 chs)

Record Type 2

Customer no and suffix	1–6	(suffix = 01)
Address	7–46	(2 lines @ 20 chs)
Telephone	47–56	
Filler	57–66	

Record Type 3

Customer no and suffix	1–6	(suffix = 02–99)
Invoice no	7–12	
Date of invoice	13–18	
Value of invoice	19–24	
VAT	25–29	
Customer order no	30–39	
Date of order	40–45	
Payment/credit	46–51	
Payment/credit type	52	
Date of payment/credit	53–58	
Filler	59–66	

Fig. 7.6

```
FD CUST-FILE.
01 CUST-RECORD.
    02      CUST-KEY.
            03 CUST-NO                      PIC 9(4).
            03 CUST-SUFFIX                  PIC 99.
    02      CUST-TYPE-1.
            03 CUST-NAME                    PIC X(20).
            03 CUST-ADD-1                   PIC X(20).
            03 CUST-ADD-2                   PIC X(20).
    02      CUST-TYPE-2 REDEFINES CUST-TYPE-1.
            03 CUST-ADD-3                   PIC X(20).
            03 CUST-ADD-4                   PIC X(20).
            03 CUST-TELE                    PIC X(10).
            03 FILLER                       PIC X(10).
    02      CUST-TYPE-3 REDEFINES CUST-TYPE-1.
            03 CUST-INVOICE                 PIC 9(6).
            03 CUST-INVDATE                 PIC 9(6).
            03 CUST-VALUE                   PIC 9(4)V99.
            03 CUST-VAT                     PIC 999V99.
            03 CUST-ORDER                   PIC X(10).
            03 CUST-ORDERDATE               PIC 9(6).
            03 CUST-PAYMENT                 PIC 9(4)V99.
            03 CUST-PAYTYPE                 PIC 9.
            03 CUST-PAYDATE                 PIC 9(6).
            03 FILLER                       PIC X(8).
```

Fig. 7.7

the key and 00 to the suffix. This would be followed by successive sequential reads until a change of customer is encountered. This is illustrated in Fig. 7.8.

An alternative approach might be to use the START statement instead of the initial read by key. This would be written

START CUST-FILE = CUST-KEY INVALID KEY . . .

The START statement is used to position randomly the record pointer to the first of a series of records. To make the first record available to the program a sequential Read must be issued after the START statement. The rest of the series will also be accessed sequentially. The file must be specified as ACCESS IS SEQUENTIAL (or ACCESS IS DYNAMIC). The use of RANDOM is illegal because the use of the START statement implies subsequent

```
ENVIRONMENT DIVISION.
            .
            .
FILE-CONTROL.
        SELECT CUST-FILE ASSIGN "CUST.DAT"
                ORGANIZATION INDEXED ACCESS DYNAMIC
                RECORD KEY CUST-KEY.
            .
            .
DATA DIVISION.
FILE SECTION.
FD CUST-FILE
            .
            .
WORKING-STORAGE SECTION.
            .
        02 CUSTOMER               PIC 9(4)
            .
PROCEDURE DIVISION.
            .
            .
        OPEN INPUT CUST-FILE.
            .
        MOVE CUSTOMER TO CUST-NO.
        MOVE 00 TO CUST-SUFFIX.
        READ CUST-FILE INVALID KEY...
            .
            .
READ-NEXT-CUSTOMER.
        READ CUST-FILE AT END...
        IF CUST-NO NOT = CUSTOMER...
            .
            .
        GO TO READ-NEXT-CUSTOMER.
```

Fig. 7.8

sequential retrieval of data records. Note that the file itself must be open in INPUT or I-O mode.

In the example of a START statement given above the system uses the data item CUST-KEY, which is the record key as defined in the SELECT statement. However, it would be possible to use another data item as the key, and that data item need not be the same length as the record key. This is illustrated in Fig. 7.9.

There we use the word KEY to specify that a data item other than the record key is to be used as key to the file. The fact that CUST-NO is just part of the record key will result in the remainder of the key (CUST-SUFFIX) being ignored in the search for the record. The START statement will find the first entry with the required customer number irrespective of the suffix. For the purposes of record

```
ENVIRONMENT DIVISION.
            .
            .
FILE-CONTROL.
      SELECT CUST-FILE ASSIGN "CUST.DAT"
            ORGANIZATION INDEXED ACCESS DYNAMIC
            RECORD KEY CUST-KEY.
            .
            .
DATA DIVISION.
FILE SECTION.
FD CUST-FILE.
01 CUST-RECORD.
      02      CUST-KEY.
            03 CUST-NO           PIC 9(4)
            03 CUST-SUFFIX       PIC 99.
      02      ...
            .
WORKING-STORAGE SECTION.
            .
            .
      02      CUSTOMER           PIC 9(4)

PROCEDURE DIVISION.
            .
      OPEN INPUT CUST-FILE.
            .
      MOVE CUSTOMER TO CUST-NO.
      MOVE Ø Ø TO CUST-SUFFIX.
      START CUST-FILE KEY: CUST-NO.
      INVALID KEY...
READ-NEXT-CUSTOMER.
      READ CUST-FILE AT END...
      IF CUST-NO NOT = CUSTOMER...
            .
      GO TO READ-NEXT-CUSTOMER.
```

Fig. 7.9

78

searching, the START statement permits comparisons on the basis of greater than and less than as well as on equality.

Just as records may be read requentially and/or randomly, so they may be written sequentially and/or randomly. In order to write a record, the file must be opened in OUTPUT or I-O (INPUT-OUTPUT) mode. The rule governing the sequence of records to be written are similar to those governing the reading of records; that is, if the file is selected as ACCESS IS SEQUENTIAL records must be presented for writing to disc in record key sequence. However, if ACCESS IS RANDOM or DYNAMIC records may be written in any sequence.

There may also be times when it is desired to read a record, modify it and then rewrite it. In this case the file must be open in I-O mode. The procedures for file handling will depend on whether the file is selected for access in sequential mode or in random (or dynamic) mode.

The rules for rewriting sequentially accessed files are:

(a) the record must be read sequentially;
(b) the contents of the record may be changed, though the record key must remain unaltered; and
(c) the record is rewritten by means of the REWRITE statement. An INVALID KEY phrase must be used. This will be invoked if the record key of the record being rewritten is not the same as that of the last record read.

For random and dynamic modes of access to files, the rewritten record may have a key different from that of the last record read. In that event, the old record read will remain on the file and a new record will be created with the new key.

The DELETE instruction is used to make a record unavailable for further access. The record is not physically removed from the file; it is simply tagged by the system as being unavailable. That is the deletion is a logical, and not a physical, deletion.

In order to delete a record from a file logically, the file must be open in I-O mode. For a file specified as ACCESS IS SEQUENTIAL, the last file handling instruction executed for the file must have been a successful read; and it is that last record read which is deleted. The coding used might be as shown in Fig. 7.10. Note that the INVALID path is not specified for sequential access deletions.

Where the file is defined as ACCESS IS RANDOM (or DYNAMIC) the record does not have to be read prior to deletion. The system will attempt to delete the record specified in the record key. If

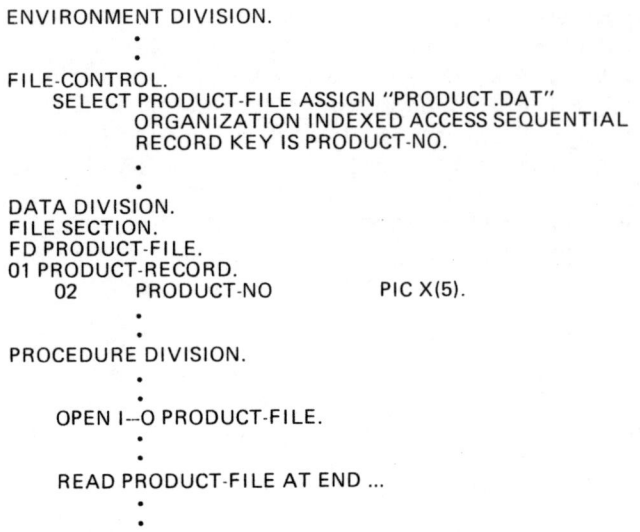

```
ENVIRONMENT DIVISION.
            .
            .
FILE-CONTROL.
     SELECT PRODUCT-FILE ASSIGN "PRODUCT.DAT"
          ORGANIZATION INDEXED ACCESS SEQUENTIAL
          RECORD KEY IS PRODUCT-NO.
            .
            .
DATA DIVISION.
FILE SECTION.
FD PRODUCT-FILE.
01 PRODUCT-RECORD.
     02      PRODUCT-NO           PIC X(5).
            .
            .
PROCEDURE DIVISION.
            .
            .
     OPEN I--O PRODUCT-FILE.
            .
            .
     READ PRODUCT-FILE AT END ...
            .
            .
     DELETE PRODUCT-FILE.
```

Fig. 7.10

the record does not exist, the INVALID path is followed. The coding might look like that shown in Fig. 7.11.

After the completion of file processing, the file must be closed. The format is

CLOSE filename.

It is important to remember that failure to close a file previously opened in OUTPUT mode could lead to the corruption of the file.

Reorganization of indexed files

Where an indexed file is volatile it may be necessary to reorganise the file quite frequently. By volatile, we mean where the file is subject to a relatively large measure of change in the form of insertions and deletions.

As was illustrated in Chapter 3, the data part of an indexed file is stored on disc in the sequence in which the records were written. Only if the file was created sequentially would the records be stored in record key sequence; and subsequent insertion of records results in the placing of the new records at the back end of the file. The index part of the file handles access to particular records and

```
ENVIRONMENT DIVISION.
        •
        •
FILE-CONTROL.
      SELECT PRODUCT-FILE ASSIGN "PRODUCT.DAT"
            ORGANIZATION INDEXED ACCESS RANDOM
            RECORD KEY IS PRODUCT-NO.

DATA DIVISION.
FILE SECTION.
FD PRODUCT-FILE.
01 PRODUCT-RECORD.
      02      PRODUCT-NO            PIC X(5)
        •
        •
PROCEDURE DIVISION.
        •
        •
      OPEN I—O PRODUCT-FILE
        •
        •
      MOVE ... TO PRODUCT-NO.
      DELETE PRODUCT-FILE INVALID-KEY ...
```

Fig. 7.11

sequencing. If the data records are not in record key sequence, random access to particular records may be slow; and even sequential access may be slow, especially if the key is long.

Deleted records also introduce inefficiency into the system because they are merely tagged and not physically removed from the file. They therefore occupy disc storage space and are read by the system even though they are subsequently ignored.

The normal method of reorganisation is to unload and reload the index file. The unload process entails running a program which reads the index file sequentially and writes the records to a sequential file. Figure 7.12 is an example of the process.

The sequential file will be held in the record key sequence of the indexed file, but will not contain any of the deleted records. The sequential file is then read and the index file created sequentially, as shown in Fig. 7.13.

The effects of whether the data portion is stored in key sequence or a random order on the timing of runs may be illustrated by means of a simple example. A product file containing 675 records was created in the format specified in the list program shown in Chapter 1. The initial creation put the records onto the file in random order.

The list program was run on a daisywheel printer which operates at 43 characters per second. This produced a list in record key sequence. The total running time was 17 minutes and 10 seconds. The file was then unloaded to a line sequential file in 5 minutes 35

81

```
010000 IDENTIFICATION DIVISION.
010100 PROGRAM-ID.    UNLOAD.
010200 ENVIRONMENT DIVISION.
010300 CONFIGURATION SECTION.
010400 SOURCE-COMPUTER.    MODEL-XYZ.
010500 OBJECT-COMPUTER.    MODEL-XYZ.
010600 INPUT-OUTPUT SECTION.
010700 FILE-CONTROL.
010800     SELECT PRODUCT-FILE ASSIGN TO "PRODUCT.DAT"
010900         ORGANIZATION INDEXED   ACCESS SEQUENTIAL
011000         RECORD KEY   PRODUCT-KEY.
011100     SELECT OUT-FILE ASSIGN TO "TEMP.DAT"
011200         ORGANIZATION LINE SEQUENTIAL.
020000 DATA DIVISION.
020100 FILE SECTION.
020200 FD   PRODUCT-FILE.
020300 01   PRODUCT-REC.
020400     02   PRODUCT-KEY    PIC X(5).
020500     02   FILLER         PIC X(36).
020600 FD   OUT-FILE.
020700 01   OUT-REC   PIC X(41).
030000 PROCEDURE DIVISION.
030100 BEGIN.
030200     OPEN INPUT PRODUCT-FILE
030300          OUTPUT OUT-FILE.
030400 READ-PRODUCT.
030500     READ PRODUCT-FILE AT END GO TO FINISH.
030600     MOVE PRODUCT-REC TO OUT-REC.
030700     WRITE OUT-REC.
030800     GO TO READ-PRODUCT.
030900 FINISH.
031000     CLOSE PRODUCT-FILE OUT-FILE.
031100     STOP RUN.
```

Fig. 7.12

seconds and reloaded in record key sequence in a further 14 minutes 22 seconds. The product file was now in record key sequence and the list program was rerun. This time it took 15 minutes 55 seconds to run, a saving of 1 minute 15 seconds.

It must be noted, of course, that the process of file security and maintenance took a fairly long time.

Programming requirements for relative files

Whereas data records which make up sequential and indexed files are physically stored on the disc one immediately next to another, the records which constitute a relative file are stored in disc positions relative to the start of the file. The record with relative key 1 is stored in the first position, the record with relative key 2 in the second position, and so on. There may well be gaps between physical records. For example space will be allocated for the record with relative key 8

```
010000 IDENTIFICATION DIVISION.
010100 PROGRAM-ID.   LOAD.
010200 ENVIRONMENT DIVISION.
010300 CONFIGURATION SECTION.
010400 SOURCE-COMPUTER.   MODEL-XYZ.
010500 OBJECT-COMPUTER.   MODEL-XYZ.
010600 INPUT-OUTPUT SECTION.
010700 FILE-CONTROL.
010800     SELECT PRODUCT-FILE ASSIGN TO "PRODUCT.DAT"
010900        ORGANIZATION INDEXED  ACCESS SEQUENTIAL
011000          RECORD KEY  PRODUCT-KEY.
011100     SELECT IN-FILE ASSIGN TO "TEMP.DAT"
011200        ORGANIZATION LINE SEQUENTIAL.
020000 DATA DIVISION.
020100 FILE SECTION.
020200 FD   PRODUCT-FILE.         '
020300 01   PRODUCT-REC.
020400      02   PRODUCT-KEY    PIC X(5).
020500      02   FILLER         PIC X(36).
020600 FD   IN-FILE.
020700 01   IN-REC    PIC X(41).
030000 PROCEDURE DIVISION.
030100 BEGIN.
030200     OPEN INPUT IN-FILE
030300          OUTPUT PRODUCT-FILE.
030400 READ-PRODUCT.
030500     READ IN-FILE AT END GO TO FINISH.
030600     MOVE IN-REC TO PRODUCT-REC.
030700     WRITE PRODUCT-REC.
030800     GO TO READ-PRODUCT.
030900 FINISH.
031000     CLOSE PRODUCT-FILE IN-FILE.
031100     STOP RUN.
```

Fig. 7.13

even though there may be no such record.

A random file may be processed sequentially. In this case the SELECT statement must specify ACCESS SEQUENTIAL (or DYNAMIC); records will be accessed in relative key sequence. But remember that this is not necessarily the same as record key sequence, the relative key being determined by the key transformation formula used. (See Chapter 4.)

Random access to records stored in a relative file is possible if ACCESS SEQUENTIAL (or DYNAMIC) is specified. In this case the program must inform the system of the required relative key.

Figure 7.14 is an extended version of the program listed earlier (Fig. 7.5). Data is entered on the VDU screen and is written to a sequential file. During processing there is random access to a relative file, CUST.DAT. The new lines relate to:

(a) selection of the relative file (lines 001500–001700);
(b) the file description of the file (lines 003100–003400);

83

```
000100 IDENTIFICATION DIVISION.
000200 PROGRAM-ID.   ORDERS1.
000300 ENVIRONMENT DIVISION.
000400 CONFIGURATION SECTION.
000500 SOURCE-COMPUTER.   MODEL-XYZ.
000600 OBJECT-COMPUTER.   MODEL-XYZ.
000700 SPECIAL-NAMES.   CONSOLE IS CRT.
000800 INPUT-OUTPUT SECTION.
000900 FILE-CONTROL.
001000    SELECT ORDERS-FILE ASSIGN TO "ORDERS.DAT"
001100         ORGANIZATION SEQUENTIAL.
001200    SELECT PRODUCT-FILE ASSIGN TO "PRODUCT.DAT"
001300         ORGANIZATION INDEXED   ACCESS RANDOM
001400         RECORD KEY IS PRODUCT-NO.
001500    SELECT CUST-FILE ASSIGN "CUST.DAT"
001600         ORGANIZATION RELATIVE   ACCESS RANDOM
001700         RELATIVE KEY IS REL-KEY.

002000 DATA DIVISION.
002100 FILE SECTION.
002200 FD  ORDERS-FILE.
002300 01  ORDERS-RECORD.
002400     02  ORDERS-CUST   PIC 9(4).
002500     02  ORDERS-PROD   PIC X(5).
002600     02  ORDERS-QTY    PIC 9(4).
002700 FD  PRODUCT-FILE.
002800 01  PRODUCT-RECORD.
002900     02  PRODUCT-NO    PIC X(5).
003000     02  FILLER        PIC X(36).
003100 FD  CUST-FILE.
003200 01  CUST-RECORD.
003300     02  CUST-NO       PIC 9(4).
003400     02  FILLER        PIC X(120).

004000 WORKING-STORAGE SECTION.
004100 01  REL-KEY    PIC 9(4).
004200 01  DISPLAY-SCREEN.
004300     02  FILLER   PIC X(35).
004400     02  DISP-1   PIC X(11)   VALUE "ORDERS ENTRY".
004500     02  FILLER   PIC X(121).
004600     02  DISP-2   PIC X(19)   VALUE "CUSTOMER NO  ]     [".
004700     02  FILLER   PIC X(7).
004800     02  DISP-3   PIC X(18)   VALUE "PRODUCT NO ]     [".
004900     02  FILLER   PIC X(6).
005000     02  DISP-4   PIC X(15)   VALUE "QUANTITY ]     [".
005100 01  ENTER-SCREEN   REDEFINES  DISPLAY-SCREEN.
005200     02  FILLER   PIC X(181).
005300     02  SCREEN-CUST   PIC 9(4).
005400     02  FILLER    PIC X(20).
005500     02  SCREEN-PRODUCT  PIC X(5).
005600     02  FILLER    PIC X(17).
005700     02  SCREEN-QTY   PIC 9(4).
```

Fig. 7.14

(c) the description of the relative key itself (line 004100); note that
the relative key is a data item defined in the Working-Storage Section
as an integer;

```
010000 PROCEDURE DIVISION.
010100 OPEN-FILES.
010200     OPEN INPUT PRODUCT-FILE CUST-FILE
010300         OUTPUT ORDERS-FILE.
010400     DISPLAY SPACE.
010500     DISPLAY DISPLAY-SCREEN.
010600 INPUT-DATA.
010700     MOVE SPACE TO ENTER-SCREEN.
010800     DISPLAY ENTER-SCREEN.
010900     DISPLAY "                              " AT 1501.
011000 ENTER-INPUT.
011100     ACCEPT ENTER-SCREEN.
011200     IF SCREEN-CUST = 9999 GO TO FINISH.
011300     MOVE SCREEN-CUST TO REL-KEY.
011400     READ CUST-FILE INVALID KEY GO TO BAD-CUST.
011500     MOVE SCREEN-PRODUCT TO PRODUCT-NO.
011600     READ PRODUCT-FILE INVALID KEY GO TO BAD-PROD.
011700     IF SCREEN-QTY NOT NUMERIC GO TO BAD-QTY.
011800     MOVE SCREEN-CUST TO ORDERS-CUST.
011900     MOVE SCREEN-PRODUCT TO ORDERS-PROD.
012000     MOVE SCREEN-QTY TO ORDERS-QTY.
012100     WRITE ORDERS-RECORD.
012200     GO TO INPUT-DATA.
012300 BAD-CUST.
012400     DISPLAY "* INVALID CUSTOMER *" AT 1501.
012500     GO TO ENTER-INPUT.
012600 BAD-PROD.
012700     DISPLAY "* INVALID PRODUCT NO *" AT 1501.
012800     GO TO ENTER-INPUT.
012900 BAD-QTY.
013000     DISPLAY "* INVALID QUANTITY *" AT 1501.
013100     GO TO ENTER-INPUT.
013200 FINISH.
013300     CLOSE ORDERS-FILE PRODUCT-FILE CUST-FILE.
013400     STOP RUN.
```

Fig. 7.14 Cont.

(d) the OPEN statement (line 010200) which opens the file as an input file;
(e) the setting up of the relative key prior to the read and the read statement itself (lines 011200–011400). The read uses the INVALID KEY option to cater for situations where no data record is found.

Relative file organisation is often suited to the requirements of reference files, where there is a need to gain rapid access to particular records. In the example given above, the customer number acted as the relative key without any key conversion. This provides very fast random access of records, and in this case if the file were accessed sequentially it would make customer records available in customer number sequence.

For a file of this nature, where no conversion is required, the decision on whether to choose relative organisation or indexed organisation would depend largely upon the gaps between record numbers.

85

If there were few gaps, or if the gaps between record numbers small, there could be considerable advantage in using relative organisation in terms of speed and disc space utilisation. But if there were substantial gaps between the keys, indexed organisation could save disc space, though processing may be slower.

Where a complex key transformation formula is used, the problem of duplication may arise. That is, two or more data records may have their record keys converted to the same relative key. Figure 7.15 shows the programming method that might be used to handle random access to records, where there may be duplicates.

In an example, it is required to find a record with a particular six-digit colour code. The colour code is converted to a relative key by the prime number division method as explained in Chapter 4. The required code is moved to a Working-Storage data item called WANTED-CODE, and the relative key calculated by dividing WANTED-CODE by 997 and adding 1 to the remainder. A random read is then issued. If the required record is found then the normal processing can be carried out. If not, a search is made through the overflow area for the desired record. A starting relative key is set up by means of a START instruction. This is followed by successive sequential reads until either the desired record is found or end of file is reached.

The rules for deleting records and for writing and rewriting records are similar to those pertaining to indexed files in terms of permissible combinations of input-output statements, access modes and open modes.

Error handling

Normally an input-output error will result in the program being aborted. The effect on the condition of data files could then be uncertain as they will not have been closed at the time of the program failure. It is therefore desirable to have some internal control over what happens in the event of input-output errors.

Besides AT END and INVALID KEY, additional control may be exercised through the execution of a USE statement, which will form part of a special section of a program called DECLARATIVES. Declaratives may be inserted immediately after the PROCEDURE DIVISION heading and indicate the conditions under which they may be called, and the instructions to be executed. After carrying out the USE procedure, control passes back to the main program.

For example, the file which the program is trying to open may not exist. The USE could be used to enable a suitable alternative file to be specified. This is illustrated in Fig. 7.16. In this example the program begins by asking the operator to enter the file name. If the file does not exist, the error at the time of attempting to open the file causes the declaratives section to be invoked. This sets an error flag to 'E' and returns control to the statement immediately following the

```
ENVIRONMENT DIVISION.
         .
         .
INPUT-OUTPUT SECTION.
FILE-CONTROL.
      SELECT COLOUR-FILE ASSIGN "COL.DAT"
          ORGANIZATION RELATIVE  ACCESS DYNAMIC
          RELATIVE KEY REL-KEY.
DATA DIVISION.
FILE SECTION.
FD   COLOUR-FILE.
01 COLOUR-RECORD.
      02  COLOUR-CODE    PIC 9(6).
      02  COLOUR-NAME    PIC X(20).
         .

WORKING-STORAGE SECTION.
77   REL-KEY     PIC 9(4).
77   WANTED-CODE  PIC 9(6).
77   DEC     PIC V999.
         .
PROCEDURE DIVISION.
         .
      OPEN INPUT COLOUR-FILE.
         .
         .
      MOVE ... TO WANTED-CODE.
      DIVIDE 997 INTO WANTED-CODE GIVING DEC.
      MULTIPLY DEC BY 997 GIVING REL-KEY ROUNDED.
      ADD 1 TO REL-KEY.
      READ COLOUR-FILE  INVALID KEY GO TO START-DUPLICATE-SEARCH.
      IF COLOUR-CODE = WANTED-CODE GO TO PROCESS-COLOUR.
START-DUPLICATE-SEARCH.
      MOVE 1000 TO REL-KEY.
      START COLOUR-FILE INVALID KEY GO TO NO-MATCH.
      GO TO READ-DUPLICATE.
TEST-DUPLICATE.
      IF COLOUR-CODE = WANTED-CODE GO TO PROCESS-COLOUR.
READ-DUPLICATE.
      READ COLOUR-FILE AT END GO TO NO-MATCH.
      GO TO TEST-DUPLICATE.
PROCESS-COLOUR.
         .
         .            procedure where required record is found
         .
NO-MATCH.
         .
         .            no matching record on file
         .
```

Fig. 7.15

```
ENVIRONMENT DIVISION.
        .
        SELECT DAY-FILE ASSIGN FILE-NAME
                ORGANIZATION SEQUENTIAL.
        .
DATA DIVISION.
FILE SECTION.
FD  DAY-FILE.
        .
        .
        .
WORKING-STORAGE SECTION.
01  FILE-NAME    PIC X(8).
01  ERR-FLAG     PIC X   VALUE SPACE.
01  INPUT-NAME   PIC X(26) VALUE
        "Enter file name ]          [".
01  ACCEPT-INPUT   REDEFINES   INPUT-NAME.
        02  FILLER       PIC X(17).
        02  ACC-FILE     PIC X(8).
        .
        .
PROCEDURE DIVISION.
DECLARATIVES.
OPEN-ERROR SECTION.   USE AFTER ERROR PROCEDURES ON DAY-FILE.
SET-ERR-TAG.
        MOVE "E" TO ERR-FLAG.
END DECLARATIVES.
BEGIN.
        .
        .
        DISPLAY INPUT-NAME.
        ACCEPT ACCEPT-INPUT.
MOVE-NAME.
        MOVE ACC-FILE TO FILE-NAME.
        OPEN INPUT DAY-FILE.
        IF ERR-TAG = "E" GO TO BEGIN.
        .
        .
```

Fig. 7.16

open. If the error flag is set to 'E', the program once again asks for
the name of the required input file.

The following points should be noted about the use of declaratives
for file handling:

(a) all declaratives are placed immediately after the PROCEDURE
DIVISION entry, starting with the header DECLARATIVES.
(b) The declaratives part of the program consists of one or more sections. Each section has a name (OPEN-ERROR SECTION is one
in the example) and has an associated USE statement written on the
same line as the section name, and ending in a period followed by a
space.

88

(c) the USE statement itself is not executed. It merely defines the conditions under which the procedures following it are carried out. The actual procedures are written in the paragraph(s) following the USE statement.

(d) The procedures in declaratives that are executed may use any normal COBOL statements apart from file handling instructions. (i.e. OPEN, CLOSE, READ, WRITE etc. must not be used.)

(e) The procedures in declaratives must not reference any procedure name (i.e. paragraph or section name) in the main body of the Procedure Division.

(f) After carrying out the procedures laid down in declaratives, control passes to the routine which caused the error or exception condition.

(g) The declaratives part of the Procedure Division ends with the entry END DECLARATIVES. The main body of the Procedure Division then follows.

Summary

The chapter explained the COBOL procedures for handling these types of file. In particular it showed how reference to files involved three Divisions of the COBOL program, from initial file selection and definition of the form of organisation and access, through the description of the records which make up the file, to the opening, closing and other input-output processing of the file. The interlinking of file references was shown to be on a number of levels:

(a) the COBOL source program names have to be identical across all references to the file;

(b) the method of file organisation can impose limitations on the procedures to be carried out, for example sequential files can be accessed in sequential mode only;

(c) the mode of access, whether sequential, random or dynamic, imposes limitations upon the sequencing of access to records.

The need to specify the name of the required file, as held on the disc directory, was shown, though some element of flexibility could be introduced to enable the decision of the actual file to be used to be left until the program was being run.

The possibility of programmer control over action to be taken in the event of error conditions was explained.

Self-test questions

1 What type of file may be open in EXTEND mode, and what is the function of EXTEND mode?

2 An indexed file has the customer number as the record key. The keys of the first few records are

AA001
AA002
AA100
AA104
AB016
AB110
AC045

(a) Processing is to start at AB016 and then continue in sequence. Show the Procedure Division coding required to achieve this.

(b) AC045 is moved to the record key and a START instruction given. What are the contents of the record area immediately after the START is executed?

(c) What ACCESS mode must be specified in the file SELECT statement?

3 A file is selected as ORGANIZATION RELATIVE. If the ACCESS mode is SEQUENTIAL will the records be accessed in record key sequence?

4 A DELETE instruction is given to a relative file. What effect does this have on the file storage space on disc?

5 If a DELETE is given to a record stored on an indexed file what effect is there on the file storage space?

6 It is required to print a total on a page in such a way as to make it stand out. What series of instructions allows overprinting to enable this to be achieved?

7 Why may it be necessary to reorganize an indexed file? How might the reorganization be done?

8 What coding may be introduced into a program to enable the user to select a particular file, from a range of possible files, for processing at run time?

8
Arithmetic and data handling

The data manipulation procedures comprise arithmetic and other manipulation and editing of the contents of data fields.

There are three main forms of data manipulation statement: arithmetic procedures; movement of data from one field to another, perhaps incorporating some editing; and manipulation of the contents of a data item.

Arithmetic

There are four basic arithmetic procedures: ADD, SUBTRACT, MULTIPLY and DIVIDE. In addition, some COBOL compilers allow for more complex arithmetic procedures through the use of the COMPUTE statement.

Arithmetic may be performed only on fields which are defined as numeric and which contain numeric data. However, the operands need not have identical data descriptions because COBOL automatically aligns decimal points and takes signs and data formats into account. Thus it is also permitted to do arithmetic where one field is held in binary, another in packed decimal form and a third field in character format.

The maximum size of each field is 18 characters. The result field may, if required, be rounded. Exceptional results which exceed the size limit of the result field can be treated as errors through the SIZE ERROR clause which may be associated with each of the arithmetic verbs.

ADD

The ADD verb allows the contents of two or more fields to be summed, and the result placed in one or more data fields. There are two major formats:

(a) The simplest form might read

ADD FIELD-1 TO FIELD-1.

The two fields are first decimal point aligned and then summed. In the example above the result is put into FIELD-2. The effect is as follows:

FIELD-1 PICTURE	Contents	FIELD-1 PICTURE	Contents before	Contents after
99	24	99	17	41
99	24	99V9	17.5	41.5
99V9	24.5	99	17	41

It is permitted to add a numeric literal to a data field, so long as no attempt is made to treat the literal as the receiving field. Thus ADD 1 TO TOTAL is permitted, whereas ADD TOTAL TO 1 is illegal.

Three fields may be summed and the result put into the last-named field while leaving the contents of the other two fields unchanged. For example

ADD TOTAL-1 TOTAL-2 TO TOTAL-3

TOTAL-1 PIC	Contents	TOTAL-2 PIC	Contents	TOTAL-3 PIC	Content Before	Content after
99V9	12.8	99V9	17.8	99	34	64

Rounding may be taken into account as follows

ADD TOTAL-1 TOTAL-2 TO TOTAL-3 ROUNDED

In the example above, where TOTAL-1 TOTAL-2 and TOTAL-3 contain 12.8, 17.8 and 34 respectively, the effect of the ROUNDED clause is that the final result is stored in TOTAL-3 as 65.

(b) It may be that the final result is to be placed in a field whose contents were not part of the adding procedure. This is achieved as follows:

ADD FIELD-1 FIELD-2 GIVING FIELD-3.

In this case the contents of FIELD-1 and FIELD-2 remain unaltered. They are simply added and the sum put into FIELD-3. Note the use of the word GIVING and the absence of the word TO.

It is possible to add to two or more fields in the single statement. For example

ADD 1 TO TOTAL-1 TOTAL-2.

Here, the contents of both TOTAL-1 and TOTAL-2 are incremented by one.

Similarly, there can be two or more receiving fields through the GIVING option. For example,

ADD FIELD-1 FIELD-2 GIVING TOTAL-1 TOTAL-2.

In this case the contents of FIELD-1 and FIELD-2 are summed and the result put into both TOTAL-1 and TOTAL-2.

SUBTRACT

The rules for SUBTRACT are similar to those applying to ADD. Thus

SUBTRACT 10 FROM TOTAL-1

results in the contents of TOTAL-1 being decreased by 10. And

SUBTRACT 5 FIELD-1 FROM TOTAL-1

results in the sum of 5 plus the contents of FIELD-1 being subtracted from TOTAL-1 and the result stored in TOTAL-1.

The ROUNDED AND GIVING options are available and operate as in the ADD instruction.

MULTIPLY

The MULTIPLY verb enables the contents of two fields to be multiplied and the result stored in one of the fields or in a third field. For example

MULTIPLY FIELD-1 BY FIELD-2

puts the result in FIELD-2 while

MULTIPLY GROSSPAY BY TAXRATE GIVING TAX

puts the result in TAX, while leaving both GROSSPAY and TAXRATE unchanged.

As with the other arithmetic instructions, the result can be rounded if required.

DIVIDE

The DIVIDE instruction enables one data item to be divided by another. The resulting quotient is put into one or more receiving fields. For example

DIVIDE 7 INTO DAYS GIVING WEEKS.

Rounding will take place only if specified. The remainder is not directly available; if wanted, the remainder would have to be calculated by manipulating the decimal portion of the quotient. For example, the data entries may be described as

```
77  DAYS       PIC 999.
77  WEEKS      PIC 999.
77  REM-1      PIC V99.
77  REMAINDER  PIC 9.
```

and the procedure would then be

DIVIDE 7 INTO DAYS GIVING WEEKS REM-1
MULTIPLY REM-1 BY 7 GIVING REMAINDER
ROUNDED.

In the example given above we used the DIVIDE . . . INTO format. It is also permissible to use the format

DIVIDE TOTAL BY COUNTER GIVING AVERAGE.

COMPUTE

This verb is currently not available on certain versions of microcomputer COBOL such as CIS COBOL, though it is available on versions of the language for the Tandy TRS-80.

The basic format would look like

COMPUTE   TRANSACT   ROUNDED = PRICE   *
QUANTITY

Unlike the other arithmetic statements, the COMPUTE specifies the receiving data item first, followed by the word 'EQUALS' or 'FROM' or the symbol '=', and finally the arithmetic expression or formula. Note that the asterisk here denotes multiplication.

There may be several receiving data items, for example

COMPUTE AREA-1 ROUNDED AREA-2 = LENGTH *
BREADTH.

This will cause the values in LENGTH and BREADTH to be multiplied and the result put into both AREA-1 (rounded) and AREA-2 (unrounded).

94

The arithmetic expression can be of any degree of complexity. For example

COMPUTE VAL-1 = ((PRICE * QTY) + SURCHARGE) * 1.15.

The parentheses are used as a control mechanism. Thus the contents of PRICE and QTY are multiplied and the contents of SURCHARGE added to the result. This resulting value is then multiplied by 1.15 and the final result is put into VAL-1.

The system will generate intermediate data fields to hold values of parts of the arithmetic expression. The intermediate data fields are generated as elementary items with a PICTURE S9(18)V9(18), that is with 18 digits both before and after the assumed decimal point. Greater precision is not available.

SIZE ERROR option

Each of the arithmetic verbs has the SIZE ERROR phrase available. This phrase allows the programmer to specify action to be taken if the result contains more digits to the left of the decimal point than specified in the receiving data area. For example

MULTIPLY PRICE BY QUANTITY GIVING VAL ROUNDED.

PRICE	QUANTITY	VAL
22	54	1188

If VAL is defined as PIC 999, that is as a three-digit data item, the result of the arithmetic would be too large to fit into it. Without the SIZE ERROR option, the contents of VAL is designated 'undefined', though it would probably contain 188, and there would be nothing to indicate that an error had occurred.

However, if the SIZE ERROR phrase is specified, then the receiving data item remains unaltered, that is it contains the value it held before the start of the arithmetic statement, and the program executes the instruction following the SIZE ERROR phrase. For example

MULTIPLY PRICE BY QUANTITY GIVING VAL ROUNDED SIZE ERROR GO TO RESULT-TOO-BIG.

In this case, if VAL is too small to hold the full result the SIZE ERROR option is invoked and the next instruction is taken from the procedure-name called RESULT-TOO-BIG.

Note that the SIZE ERROR checks only for sufficient number of receiving characters to the left of the decimal point. It should also be noted that an attempt to divide by zero will cause a SIZE ERROR condition.

Data movement and editing

Data may be moved from one data field to another, with editing taking place automatically. The format is

MOVE data-item TO identifier.

The data item to be moved may be a literal or the contents of a data field. But note that the sending and receiving fields must be compatible; thus is is not permitted to move numeric information into alphabetic data fields.

For example

MOVE 15 TO COMMISSION-RATE

is acceptable provided that COMMISSION-RATE is not defined as alphabetic (i.e. a PIC A field).

It is permitted to have several receiving fields, each of which may have different editing characteristics. For example

MOVE SALES TO VAL-1 VAL-2 VAL-3 VAL-4.

The resulting contents of VAL-1, VAL-2, VAL-3 and VAL-4 will depend upon their PICTURE definitions, and, of course, the contents of SALES.

Suppose SALES contains the value 15.25 and

VAL-1 is defined as PIC 999V99
VAL-2 is 99
VAL-3 is V99 and
VAL-4 is ZZZ.99

then the results will be

VAL-1 will contain 015.25 (assumed, not actual decimal point)
VAL-2 will contain 15
VAL-3 will contain .25 (with assumed decimal point) and
VAL-4 will contain 15.25 (with actual decimal point).

The value which is sent may also be a figurative constant; for example

MOVE SPACE TO PRINT-LINE.

or

MOVE ZERO TO TOTALS-FIELD.

Data movement is subject to rules of editing. Legality of movement from one data item to another will depend upon the classes of
both the sending and the receiving data items. The rules are summa-
rised in Fig. 8.1 and explained below.

Category of Sending Data Item	Category of Receiving Data Item		
	Alphabetic	Alphanumeric Edited Alpha- numeric	Numeric Integer, Numeric Non-Integer Numeric Edited
Alphabetic	Yes	Yes	No
Alphanumeric	Yes	Yes	Yes
Alphanumeric Edited	Yes	Yes	No
Numeric Integer	No	Yes	Yes
Numeric Non-Integer	No	No	Yes
Numeric Edited	No	Yes	Yes

Fig. 8.1 Rules of editing

(i) Alphabetic to alphabetic assumes that the PICTUREs of both
sending and receiving data items are defined as alphabetic. For
example

02   FIELD-SEND   PIC A(4).
02   FIELD-RECEIVE   PIC A(3).

MOVE FIELD-SEND TO FIELD-RECEIVE.

Standard alignment rules are followed. That is, if the sending data
item is larger than the receiving data items, the excess characters are
truncated at the right-hand end; if the receiving data item is larger,
the surplus characters at the right-hand end of the receiving data
item are space-filled.

Thus if FIELD-SEND is defined as PIC A(4) and contains
'FRED', and FIELD-RECEIVE is defined as PIC A(2), the move
will result in the contents of FIELD-RECEIVE being set to 'FR',
whereas if FIELD-RECEIVE is defined as PIC A(6) the contents
after the move would be " FRED ".

(ii) Alphabetic to alphanumeric assumes that the PICTURE of

the sending item is A, while that of the receiving data item is X. The alignment rules are as described in (i) above.

(iii) Alphabetic to alphanumeric edited. Allowable alphanumeric edited PICTURE symbols are 'A' 'X' '9' 'B' '0' and '/'. The 'B' '0' and '/' are insertion characters, and are inserted in the corresponding positions in the receiving data item. For example

```
02   FIELD-SEND      PIC A(4)   VALUE 'FRED'
02   FIELD-RECEIVE   PIC XXBXBX.
```

FIELD-RECEIVE is thus defined as a six-character data item, with blanks to be inserted into the third and fifth positions. The result of a move of the contents of FIELD-SEND to FIELD-RECEIVE is that FIELD-RECEIVE will contain the value 'FR E D'.

If FIELD-RECEIVE were defined as PIC XXX0X, it would be a five-character data item, and the result of a move from FIELD-SEND would be that it would contain the value 'FRE0D'.

As mentioned in (i) above, there can be truncation or space-fill at the right-hand end of the receiving data item if there is a shortage (or surplus) of X characters in the receiving data item's PICTURE.

(iv) Alphanumeric to alphabetic assumes that the sending data item is defined as PIC X and that of the receiving data item as PIC A. The alignment rules are as in (i) above.

(v) Alphanumeric to alphanumeric movement rules are as in (i) above.

(vi) Alphanumeric to alphanumeric edited movement rules are as in (iii) above.

(vii) Alphanumeric to numeric integer. This assumes that that sending data item is defined as PIC X and contains numeric data only. For example

```
02   FIELD-SEND      PIC X(4)   VALUE "1234".
02   FIELD-RECEIVE   PIC 9(4).
```

The instruction MOVE FIELD-SEND TO FIELD-RECEIVE is legal in this case. The actual contents of the receiving data item will depend upon the value of the contents of the sending data item and the lengths of the two data items concerned. If the sending data item is the shorter of the two there will be zero-filling of the surplus characters at the left-hand end of the receiving data item. For example

```
02   FIELD-SEND      PIC X(4)   VALUE "1234".
02   FIELD-RECEIVE   PIC 9(5).
```

The result of a move is that FIELD-RECEIVE will be set to the value 01234.

If the receiving data item is shorter, there will be truncation at the left-hand end. For example

```
02   FIELD-SEND      PIC X(4)   VALUE "1234".
02   FIELD-RECEIVE   PIC 9(3).
```

The result of a move is that FIELD-RESULT will contain 234.

If the data being sent contains non-numeric characters, the result of the move is unspecified.

(viii) Alphanumeric to numeric non-integer assumes that the sending data item is defined as PIC X, and that the receiving data item contains an assumed decimal point. As in (vii) above the contents of the sending data item must be numeric. Alignment takes place initially on the assumed decimal point of the receiving data item; the contents of the sending data item are moved right to left starting immediately to the left of the assumed decimal point with zero-fill or truncation; the character positions to the right of the assumed decimal point are set to zero. For example

```
02   FIELD-SEND      PIC X(4)   VALUE "1234".
02   FIELD-RECEIVE   PIC 9(6)V99.
```

FIELD-RECEIVE is thus defined as an eight-character data item with an assumed decimal point between the sixth and seventh character positions. The result of a move of the contents of FIELD-SEND to FIELD-RECEIVE is that FIELD-RECEIVE will be set to 00123400.

(ix) Alphanumeric to numeric edited assumes that the data being sent is a numeric integer, though the data item is defined as PIC X. The rules governing the sending of data to numeric edited fields is explained in (xv) and (xvi) below.

(x) Alphanumeric edited to alphabetic, and alphanumeric edited to alphanumeric, assumes that the data being sent contains an edited value—a blank, zero, or stroke. The characters, including the edited value, are moved from the sending area to the receiving area from left to right with space-fill or truncation at the right-hand end if the data items are of different sizes. For example

```
02   FIELD-SEND PIC XXBXX.   —contains AB CD
02   FIELD-RECEIVE PIC X(4).
```

A move will result in FIELD-RECEIVE being set to AB C.

(xi) Alphanumeric edited to alphanumeric edited will result in a further element of editing. For example

```
02   FIELD-SEND      PIC XX/XX/XX.—contains AB/
CD/EF.
02   FIELD-RECEIVE   PIC XXX/BXXX.
```

The result of a move is that the contents of FIELD-RECEIVE will be AB//CD/. In this example each of the characters which make up FIELD-SEND, including the /, is moved to its corresponding X position in FIELD-RECEIVE with additional editing provided by the B and / editing symbols.

(xii) Numeric integer or alphanumeric moves are from left to right with truncation or space-fill at the right-hand end of the receiving data item if the sizes of the data items differ. For example

```
02   VAL-SEND        PIC 9(4)   VALUE 1234.
02   ALPH-RECEIVE    PIC X(5).
```

The result of a move is that ALPH-RECEIVE will contain 1234. If ALPH-RECEIVE is defined as PIC XXX, the move will cause it to contain the value 123.

(xiii) Numeric integer to numeric integer. Both fields are defined as PIC 9 and may be signed. The receiving data item will receive the sign only if it is defined as a signed field. The two data items may have different usages, in which case there will be automatic conversion at the time of the move. For example

```
02   FIELD-SEND      PIC S9(4).
02   FIELD-RECEIVE   PIC S9(4) COMP.
```

will cause the data to be converted from DISPLAY format to pure binary form when it is moved to FIELD-RECEIVE.

If the data items are of unequal sizes there will be zero-fill or truncation at the left-hand end.

(xiv) Numeric integer to numeric non-integer. The data items are aligned on the assumed decimal point of the receiving data item, with the assumed decimal point of the sending integer data item being immediately to the right of the rightmost character.

The data is moved from right to left in the integer portion of the receiving data item with zero-fill or truncation at the left-hand end if necessary, The decimal part of the receiving data items is set to zero. For example

```
02   VAL-SEND        PIC 9(4)   VALUE 1234.
02   VAL-RECEIVE     PIC 9(4)V99.
```

The move will cause the contents of VAL-RECEIVE to be set to 123400.

(xv) Numeric integer to numeric edited. There are several forms of numeric editing.

(a) Simple zero suppression, where leading zeros are replaced by spaces. For example

```
02   VAL-SEND   PIC 9(4)   VALUE 0101.
02   VAL-ED     PIC Z(4).
```

A move will result in the contents of VAL-ED being set to 101. The Z is a replacement symbol, and causes the replacement of a leading zero with a space in the corresponding position.

(b) Cheque protection zero suppression, where leading zeros are replaced by asterisks. For example

```
02   VAL-SEND   PIC 9(4)   VALUE 0012.
02   VAL-ED     PIC *(4).
```

A move will result in VAL-ED being set to **12.

(c) Fixed currency sign, where the currency sign is inserted into the corresponding position of the receiving data item. For example

```
02   VAL-SEND   PIC 9(4)   VALUE 0123.
02   VAL-ED     PIC £9(4).
```

will cause VAL-ED to be set to £0123 as a result of the move.

Cheque protection and simple zero suppression can be included in a numeric edited data item with fixed currency sign. For example

```
02   VAL-SEND   PIC 9(4)   VALUE 0120.
02   VAL-ED     PIC £*(4).
```

A move will result in the value stored in VAL-ED being set to £*120 as a result of the move.

(d) Floating currency sign. In this option the currency sign is used to suppress leading zeros and will be placed in the receiving data item immediately to the left of the first non-zero. For example

```
02   VAL-SEND   PIC 9(4)   VALUE 0120.
02   VAL-ED     PIC £(5).
```

A move will result in VAL-ED being set to £120.

(e) Debit/credit sign. DB and CR represent two character positions in determining the size of the data item, and are put at the right-hand end of the receiving data item if the value is regative. For example

```
02   VAL-SEND   PIC S9(4)   VALUE +1234.
02   VAL-ED     PIC 9(4)DB.
```

A move will cause VAL-ED to be set to 1234. However, if the contents of VAL-SEND were −1234, VAL-ED would be set to 1234DB.

It is important to note that DB and CR occupy fixed positions in the receiving data item, and these positions cannot be overwritten by data values. For example

```
02   VAL-SEND   PIC S9(4)   VALUE +1234.
02   VAL-ED      PIC 99DB.
```

A move will cause VAL-ED to contain 34 although the data item occupies four character positions. This is because fixed editing characters take precedence over data characters.

(f) + sign. This can be put at the right-hand end of the PICTURE declaration to act as a fixed insertion character. This works as follows:

```
02   VAL-SEND   PIC S9(4)   VALUE +1234.
02   VAL-ED      PIC S9(4)+.
```

A move will set VAL-ED to 1234+. But

```
02   VAL-SEND   PIC S9(4)   VALUE −1234.
02   VAL-ED      PIC 9(4)+.
```

will result in VAL-ED being set to 1234−.

The + sign can be placed at the left-hand end of the PICTURE declaration of the receiving data item. For example

```
02   VAL-SEND   PIC S9(4)   VALUE +1234.
02   VAL-ED      PIC +9(4).
```

In this case a move will cause the characters +1234 to be placed in VAL-ED.

The + can be used as a floating editing symbol, replacing leading zeros. For example

```
02   VAL-SEND   PIC S9(4)   VALUE 0012.
02   VAL-ED      PIC +(5).
```

A move will result in VAL-ED being set to   +12.

The point to remember is that if the value received is positive a + will be inserted; if the value received is negative a − will be inserted.

(g) − sign. This works in much the same way as the + insertion symbol except that if the value received is positive the + sign is not inserted.

(h) comma. This can be used as an insertion character as follows

```
02   VAL-SEND   PIC 9(5)   VALUE 12345.
02   VAL-ED        PIC 99,999.
```

A move will result in VAL-ED being set to 12, 345.

(i) Stroke (/). This may be used as an insertion character as follows:

```
02   DATE          PIC 9(6)   VALUE 040582.
02   DATE-ED   PIC 99/99/99.
```

A move will cause DATE-ED to contain the characters 04/05/82.

(xvi) Numeric non-integer to numeric edited. The options and rules listed under (xv) above apply. In addition, the assumed decimal point may be replaced by an actual decimal point. For example

```
02   VAL-SEND   PIC 99V99.   —contains 12.34
   02   VAL-ED        PIC 99.99.
```

A move will align the data items on decimal points (assumed in the case of VAL-SEND and actual in the case of VAL-ED). The data to the left of the decimal point is moved from right to left, while the data to the right of the decimal point is move from left to right. As a result of the move VAL-ED will contain 12.34.

If the receiving data item is larger than the sending data item at either side of the decimal place, the surplus characters are zero-filled. If the receiving data item is shorter at either side of the decimal place truncation will take place. So

```
02   VAL-SEND   PIC 999V999.—contains 123.456.
02   VAL-ED        PIC 99.99.
```

A move from VAL-SEND TO VAL-ED will set the contents of VAL-ED to 23.45.

(xvii) Numeric edited to alphanumeric will cause the contents of the sending data item to be moved character by character from left to right, with space fill or truncation at the right-hand end if required. For example

```
02   DATE-ED   PIC 99/99/99.—contents 04/05/82.
02   ALPHA-RECEIVE   PIC X(6).
```

A move from DATE-ED to ALPHA-RECEIVE will cause the contents to ALPH-RECEIVE to be set to 04/05/.

(xviii) Numeric edited to alphanumeric edited will cause a transfer of data as in (xvii) above, but with additional editing as specified in the PICTURE of the receiving data item. For example

    02   DATE-ED   PIC 99/99/99.—contains 04/05/82.
    02   ALPH-RECEIVE   PIC X(4)BBX(4).

A move will cause the contents of ALPH-RECEIVE to be set to 04/05/82.

(xix) Numeric edited to any type of numeric data item is permitted so long as the characters moved are numerals.

For the purposes of data movement, group items are regarded as alphanumeric data items. A move which references the group item will not convert the format of any constituent elementary item.

When figurative constants are moved, it should be remembered that ZERO belongs to category numeric and should not be moved to an alphabetic data item. Space belongs to class alphabetic and should not be moved to a numeric or numeric edited data item.

Figure 8.2 lists examples of valid moves.

Sending Data Item		Receiving Data Item	
Picture	Data	Picture	Edited Data
9(5)	12345	Z(5)	12345
9(5)	00206	Z(5)	206
9(5)	01234	£Z(5)	£1234
9(5)	01234	£(6)	£1234
9(5)	00000	£(6)	
999V99	12345	9(5)	00123
9(5)	00100	ZZ,ZZZ	100
9(5)	01000	ZZ,ZZZ	1,000
S9(5)	+12345	−Z(5)9.99	12345.00
S9(5)	−12345	−Z(5)9.99	−12345.00
S9(5)	+00123	Z(5).99DB	123.00
9(5)	12345	BB999.00	345.00
9(6)	121283	99/99/99	12/12/83
9(6)	121283	99B99B99	12 12 83
X(5)	ROBIN	X(4)BX	ROBI N
X(5)	A B C	XXBXXBX	A B C

Fig. 8.2 Examples of valid moves

Data item manipulation (the INSPECT statement)

The INSPECT statement allows the programmer to examine the contents of a data item and count and/or replace occurrences of particular characters.

Counting the number of occurences is achieved through the TALLYING phrase. For example

```
02   SURNAME   PIC X(20).—contains 'BROWN' at left-
hand end.
01   CNT        PIC 99.
   .
   .
```

INSPECT SURNAME TALLYING CNT FOR SPACE.

will set a counting action in motion, and the value 15 will be put into
the data item CNT (because SURNAME contains 'BROWN' followed by 15 spaces).

Note that the data item being 'inspected' must be a group item or
an elementary item of usage type DISPLAY. (In other words a data
item described as COMP or COMP-3 cannot be 'inspected'.) The
data item following the word TALLYING must be an elementary
numeric data item.

Again using the data items mentioned in the previous example,
the instruction might read

INSPECT SURNAME TALLYING CNT FOR ALL "A".

in which case the contents of SURNAME are examined, and the
total number of occurrences of the letter 'A' is put into CNT. If there
are no occurrences, CNT will be set to the value zero. The count can
be for the number of occurrences of a particular leading character.
For example

INSPECT SURNAME TALLYING CNT FOR LEADING
"B".

If SURNAME contains the value 'BROWN', then CNT will be set
to 1.

The count can be used to test for the existence of a group of characters. For example

INSPECT SURNAME TALLYING CNT FOR ALL "SON".

If SURNAME contains the value 'WILKINSON', the CNT will be
set to 1, whereas if it contains 'WILKINSON & SON', CNT will
be set to 2.

Additional limitations can be placed on the search through the
data item. For example

INSPECT SURNAME TALLYING CNT FOR ALL "SON"
AFTER INITIAL SPACE.

If SURNAME contains 'BROWN & SON', CNT will be set to 1, if
it contains 'WILKINSON & SON', CNT will again be set to 1.
Whereas

INSPECT SURNAME TALLYING CNT FOR ALL 'SON'
BEFORE INITIAL SPACE.

will cause CNT to be set to 1 if SURNAME contains 'WILKIN-SON & SON', but 0 if SURNAME contains 'BROWN & SON'.
This is because the search in this case ends as soon as the first blank
character is encountered in the data item.

It is permissible to make multiple tallies in the same INSPECT
statement. For example

INSPECT SURNAME TALLYING CNT FOR ALL "M"
AFTER LEADING "S", CNT-1 FOR LEADING "S"
BEFORE INITIAL "M".

If SURNAME contains 'SMITH', CNT will be set to 1 and CNT-1
to 1,

A count can be made of the number of initial non-blanks in a data
item. For example

INSPECT SURNAME TALLYING CNT FOR
CHARACTERS BEFORE INITIAL SPACE.

Replacing characters in a data item is accomplished with the
REPLACING statement. For example

INSPECT FIELD-X REPLACING ALL "0" BY SPACE.

If FIELD-X initially contains 101, the effect of the INSPECT is to
change the value to 1 1.

Or it is possible to replace a group of characters, if desired, before
or after some specified character or data item. For example

INSPECT COMPANY-NAME REPLACING ALL "LTD" BY
"PLC" AFTER INITIAL SPACE.

As in the case of tallying above, it is possible to INSPECT all characters or leading characters and replace them with some other characters. This is subject to the rule that the sizes of the data items
being inspected and the replacing data items must be the same.
Thus

INSPECT COMPANY-NAME REPLACING ALL "CO"
BY "COMPANY" AFTER INITIAL SPACE.

would be invalid, as 'CO' and 'COMPANY' are different sizes.

However, if a data item is being replaced by a figurative constant,
then the figurative constant will be assumed to be as large as the
data it replaces. For example

INSPECT NAME-X REPLACING ALL "FRED" BY SPACE.

will result in all occurrences of 'FRED' being replaced by four blanks.

It should be emphasised that where INITIAL is specified, it means the first occurrence of the character(s). For example

INSPECT FIELD-X REPLACING ALL "A" BY "E" BEFORE INITIAL 'R'.

If FIELD-X initially contains 'BARBARIC', then the contents are changed to 'BERBARIC'.

Tallying and replacing can be specified in the same INSPECT statement. This is treated as though there were two successive INSPECT statements, and is written in the form

INSPECT SURNAME TALLYING CNT FOR ALL "A" REPLACING ALL "P" BY "B".

In this case the same data item is treated to both a count of the number of occurrences of the letter 'A' and will have all occurrences of the letter 'P' replaced by 'B'.

Summary

COBOL has all the necessary facilities for handling data in a commercial environment where the emphasis is on arithmetic and data movement. Some versions of microcomputer COBOL do not as yet have the powerful COMPUTE statement, but the conventional addition, subtraction, multiplication and division statements are normally quite adequate, as is the degree of precision in the results—up to 18 decimal digits.

For data which is required to be printed, the editing facilities are far superior to those provided by any competing language for the microcomputer. Control of editing is through the description of the PICTURE clause, and editing takes place automatically when data is moved to an edited data item. This is the case whether the move is explicitly stated by a MOVE instruction, or implicit through arithmetic operations incorporating the GIVING option.

COBOL also permits the programmer to access individual characters in data items, keep a count of the number of occurrences of certain facets and, if necessary, selectively change part of the contents of the data item.

Self-test questions

1 FIELD-A is defined as PIC 9(4) and contains the value 0006.

FIELD-B is defined as PIC 9(4) and contains 0137. What will FIELD-C contain after the following instructions are executed, given the PICTURE clauses of FIELD-C in each case.

(a) FIELD-C   PIC 9(4)
        MULTIPLY FIELD-A BY FIELD-B GIVING
        FIELD-C.

(b) FIELD-C   PIC 9(4)V99.
        ADD FIELD-A FIELD-B GIVING FIELD-C.

(c) FIELD-C   PIC 9(4).
        SUBTRACT FIELD-B FROM FIELD-A GIVING
        FIELD-C.

(d) FIELD-C   PIC *(4).
        MULTIPLY FIELD-A BY FIELD-B GIVING
        FIELD-C

(e) FIELD-C   PIC £(6).
        MULTIPLY FIELD-A BY FIELD-B GIVING
        FIELD-C.

(f) FIELD-C   PIC £9(6).
        MOVE FIELD-A TO FIELD-C.

(g) FIELD-C   PIC 9PP.
        MULTIPLY FIELD-A BY FIELD-B GIVING
        FIELD-C.

2 SURNAME is defined as PIC X(12) and contains 'MALCOLM-SON'. What will be the value of TALLY as a result of each of the following statements?

(a) INSPECT SURNAME TALLYING TALLY FOR SPACE.

(b) INSPECT SURNAME TALLYING TALLY FOR LEADING SPACE.

(c) INSPECT SURNAME TALLYING TALLY FOR ALL CHARACTERS.

(d) INSPECT SURNAME TALLYING TALLY FOR ALL 'MAL'.

9

Sequence control

Procedure Division statements are normally executed in the sequence in which they are written. But there are occasions when it is necessary to depart from the normal sequence of operations. This could be as a result of:

(a) a condition test;
(b) the branch could be part of the program sequence, such as a statement at the end of a looop directing control back to the beginning of the loop; or
(c) the need to carry out a series of instructions written elsewhere in the program before continuing in sequence, i.e. performing a subroutine.

These instructions will be considered in turn.

Condition testing

The IF statement is the most common way of testing a condition within a program, and, depending upon the result of the condition test, a change of program sequence may be required. The IF statement is followed by instructions to be followed depending upon whether the condition being tested is satisfied or not.

Different versions of COBOL permit different types of condition test. The four most common types are:

1. *Comparing the contents of one data item with the contents of another.* One of the data items may be a constant or a literal. This type of test is known as a relation condition.

For example

IF TAX-WEEK GREATER 52 . . .

compares the contents of a data item called TAX-WEEK with a constant value of 52, while

IF THIS-DEPT NOT EQUAL LAST-DEPT

compares the contents of two data names.

The comparisons permitted are for equality or inequality, and greater or less than. The symbols = , < and > may be used instead of the words EQUALS, LESS and GREATER respectively.

A test for inequality requires a statement in the form

IF THIS-CODE NOT=LAST-CODE . . .

as COBOL does not recognise a symbol for inequality.

It is possible to test for a condition of less than or equals by means of the form

IF FIELD-A NOT > FIELD-B . . .

Similarly, testing for greater than or equal to is achieved through the statement in the form

IF FIELD-A NOT < FIELD-B . . .

The comparison is of type numeric only if both data items are described as unedited elementary numeric items. In such a case, both items are aligned by assumed decimal point and the values compared algebraically. The sign is taken into account in any comparison.

All other comparisons are non-numeric, irrespective of the PICTURE definitions of the data concerned. If the data items are of unequal lengths, the shorter of the two is treated as though it were space-filled at the right-hand end to make it of the same size as the other data item. Then, starting at the left-hand end, characters from both data items are compared pair by pair until inequality is found or until the end of the data items is reached.

2. *Testing the contents of a data item for a class of data (class condition).* This type of test examines the contents of a data field to see whether it is numeric or alphabetic. For example

IF IN-QTY NUMERIC . . .

causes the contents of IN-QTY to be examined to see whether it is composed entirely of numerals, that it characters in the set 0-9 (together with a sign if the data item is described as signed in the PICTURE).

The numeric test may be applied only to an elementary numeric or alphanumeric data item. It cannot be applied to any other type of elementary item nor to a group data item.

On the other hand

110

IF IN-NAME ALPHABETIC . . .

causes the contents of IN-NAME to be examined to see whether it is composed entirely of alphabetic characters and/or spaces.

For the alphabetic class test to be acceptable IN-NAME must be defined as an alphabetic data item, or an alphanumeric data item, or a group data item.

Class condition testing is commonly used for checking data or for distinguishing different types of data records. For example

```
DATA DIVISION.
FILE SECTION.
FD   CUST-FILE
01   CUST-REC-1.
     02   CUST-NAME   PIC X(20).
          :

01   CUST-REC-2.
     02   CUST-INVOICE        PIC 9(6).
     02   CUST-INVOICE-DATE   PIC 9(6).
          :

PROCEDURE DIVISION.
BEGIN.
     OPEN . . .
          :

     IF   CUST-NAME   ALPHABETIC
     GO TO NEW-CUSTOMER.
     MOVE CUST-INVOICE TO . . .
          :
```

In this example CUST-REC-1 and CUST-REC-2 occupy the same area of memory storage as different record descriptions of the same file. A test of CUST-NAME for alphabetic determines whether the record currently being processed is a new customer header or a continuation detail record.

3. *Switch-status condition.* The SPECIAL-NAMES paragraph of the Environment Division allows for the setting up program switches. CIS COBOL allows up to eight switches to be set; the switch is given a name, and condition-names are given for both ON and OFF conditions. For example

```
ENVIRONMENT DIVISION.
CONFIGURATION SECTION.
SOURCE-COMPUTER.   MODEL-XYZ.
```

```
OBJECT-COMPUTER.   MODEL-XYZ.
SPECIAL-NAMES. SWITCH 1 IS SW1 ON IS SW1-ON.
        :
PROCEDURE DIVISION.
        :
   IF SW1-ON GO TO SWITCH-1-PROCEDURE.
        :
```

The switches are initially set to off at run time. To set switch 1 on at run time the operator enters

```
RUN program-name (+1)
```

where program-name is the name of the program to be run and the entry (+1) indicates that switch 1 is to be set on.

Programmable switches are extremely useful as a means of indicating to the program the sub-sets of program and/or data to be used. For example, suppose the program is intended to calculate (and recalculate) the unit costs of production. The Product File may contain several hundred records, one per product. Each record may contain a single character field which is set to Space when the record is initially created (before the costing process) and whenever the record is amended. The costing program sets the value of that field to 'C' after the successful completion of the costing process.

The product record may be described along these lines

```
01  PRODUCT-RECORD.
    02  PRODUCT-CODE          PIC X(5).
    02  PRODUCT-DESCRIPTION   PIC X(25).
    02  PRODUCT-PROCESSES   OCCURS 4 TIMES.
        03  PRODUCT-PROC   PIC 99.
        03  PRODUCT-TIME   PIC 99.
                :
    02  PRODUCT-COST   PIC 9(4)V99.
    02  PRODUCT-TAG    PIC X.
```

Note that PRODUCT-TAG will contain Space if the record is uncosted and 'C' if it is costed.

A requirement of the program might be either to cost all product records or to cost only those records which have PRODUCT-TAG set to Space (currently uncosted). The coding might read

```
ENVIRONMENT DIVISION.
SPECIAL-NAMES. SWITCH-1 IS SW1 ON IS COST-ALL.
INPUT-OUTPUT SECTION.
```

```
        SELECT PRODUCT-FILE ASSIGN . . .
          :
DATA DIVISION.
FILE SECTION.
FD   PRODUCT-FILE.
01   PRODUCT-RECORD.
       02   PRODUCT-CODE   PIC X(5).
              :
       02   PRODUCT-TAG     PIC X.
              :
PROCEDURE DIVISION.
OPEN-FILE.
   OPEN I-O PRODUCT-FILE.
READ-RECORD.
   READ PRODUCT-FILE AT END GO TO FINISH.
   IF COST-ALL GO TO PROCESS-RECORD.
   IF PRODUCT-TAG = "C" GO TO READ-RECORD.
PROCESS-RECORD.
       :   costing procedures
       :
   MOVE "C" TO PRODUCT-TAG.
   REWRITE PRODUCT-RECORD.
   GO TO READ-RECORD.
FINISH.
   CLOSE PRODUCT-FILE.
   STOP RUN.
```

4. *The contents of signed numeric data fields may be tested for being, or not being, positive, negative or zero.* (But note that this type of condition test may not be available on all versions of microcomputer COBOL; CIS COBOL for instance does not currently provide this facility.) An example might read

   IF BALANCE NEGATIVE . . .

or

   IF TOTAL POSITIVE . . .

   Having specified one or more of the condition tests described above the programmer might specify the action to be taken in the event of the test being satisfied. It is here that the use of the period (.) is critical. There are several possible courses of action. The three principal ones are easiest explained by means of examples.

   IF FIELD-A = FIELD-B ADD 1 TO FIELD-C.
   ADD 1 TO FIELD-D.

In this case the contents of two data items, FIELD-A and FIELD-B, are compared for equality. If the test succeeds, i.e. the contents are equal, then 1 is added to the contents of FIELD-C. If the test fails, control is passed to the next sentence, i.e. the statement following the next period, in which case FIELD-C remains unaltered.

It is important to note that if the period following the word FIELD-C were omitted, then the instruction to add 1 to the contents of FIELD-D would be executed only if the condition test were satisfied, that is the contents of FIELD-A and FIELD-B were equal.

```
IF GROSSNHI < NHIMAX NEXT SENTENCE ELSE
    MOVE NHIMAX TO GROSSNHI.
MULTIPLY GROSSNHI BY NHIRATE GIVING NI.
```

In this second example, where NEXT SENTENCE is specified, if the condition being tested is satisfied, then control will pass to the next sentence (the statement following the next period). If the condition is not satisfied, the statement(s) following the word ELSE will be executed. This means that if GROSSNHI contains a value lower than in NHIMAX control passes immediately to the multiply instruction, otherwise the contents of NHIMAX are moved to GROSSNHI prior to the multiplication.

```
IF BALANCE LESS THAN ZERO ADD BALANCE TO
    TOTAL-NEGATIVE   ELSE   ADD   BALANCE   TO
    TOTAL-POSITIVE.
```

In this last example the alternative courses of action available are contained within a single sentence. If the condition is satisfied, that is if BALANCE contains a value of less than zero, the statement(s) before the word ELSE will be executed and then control passes to the next sentence; if the test fails the statement(s) following the word ELSE up to the next period will be executed.

COBOL also permits nested IF statements. For example

```
IF NHICODE = "A"
IF GROSSNHI < NHIMIN MOVE ZERO TO GROSSNHI
    ELSE
IF  GROSSNHI  >  NHIMAX  MOVE  NHIMAX  TO
    GROSSNHI.
MULTIPLY GROSSNHI BY NHIRATE GIVING NI.
```

The IF statements are treated as pairs of IF . . . ELSE combinations working from left to right. Thus in the example the comparison between GROSSNHI and NHIMAX is only made if GROSSNHI is not less than then NHIMIN. And the comparison between GROSS-NHI and NHEMIN is only carried out if NHICODE contains the

114

value 'A'. If NHICODE does not contain 'A' the other IF statements will not be executed.

Certain versions of COBOL, but not CIS COBOL at present, allow for even greater flexibility through compound condition testing by the use of AND and OR comparisons. For example

IF MONTH = 02 MOVE 28 TO DAYS ELSE
IF MONTH = 04 06 09 OR 11 MOVE 30 TO DAYS ELSE
MOVE 31 TO DAYS.

could be used as the coding which puts the number of days in the month into the data field DAYS, depending upon the month number stored in MONTH. The use of OR in the second IF statement provides for the condition being satisfied if any of the values listed are found.

Even more complex conditions may be tested. For example

IF CUST-GROUP = "A" MOVE 5 TO DISCOUNT ELSE
IF CUST-GROUP > "A" AND CUST-GROUP < "G" OR
BALANCE > 10000 MOVE 8 TO DISCOUNT ELSE
MOVE 2.5 TO DISCOUNT.

The second IF statement is converted to

IF (CUST-GROUP >"A" AND CUST-GROUP < "G") OR
BALANCE > 10000 MOVE 8 TO DISCOUNT.

In other words the value 8 is move to DISCOUNT under either of the following conditions.
(a) CUST-GROUP contains a value greater than 'A' but less than 'G'; or
(b) the contents of BALANCE exceeds 10000 (provided that CUST-GROUP is not equal to 'A').

Parentheses may be used in a compound IF statement to help ensure that the logic is entered correctly. Thus it would be permissible to rewrite the compound IF statement above as

IF CUST-GROUP = "A" MOVE 5 TO DISCOUNT ELSE
IF (CUST-GROUP > "A" AND CUST-GROUP < "G")
OR BALANCE > 10000 MOVE 8 TO DISCOUNT ELSE
MOVE 2.5 TO DISCOUNT.

Program branching

The GO TO statement is the means of transferring control from one sequence of instructions to another. Unlike the Procedure Division commands considered so far, the GO TO references a procedure name—a paragraph name or section name in the Procedure Division. For example

GO TO READ-NEXT-RECORD.

tells the run-time monitor to take as the next instruction the first statement in the paragraph called READ-NEXT-RECORD.

Note that a period must immediately follow the procedure name in the GO TO.

The format given above is an example of an unconditional GO TO, that is a change in sequence which is not dependent upon some other factor. COBOL permits the giving of a conditional GO TO. For example

    02   RECORD-TYPE   PIC 9.
          ⋮

    READ-NEXT.
        READ DATA-FILE AT END GO TO FINISH.
        GO TO TYPE-1-PROCEDURE TYPE-2-PROCEDURE
        DEPENDING ON RECORD-TYPE.
        GO TO READ-NEXT.
    TYPE-1-PROCEDURE.
          ⋮

    TYPE-2-PROCEDURE.
          ⋮

In this case the contents of data item RECORD-TYPE are examined immediately prior to the GO TO. If it contains the value 1 control will pass to the first-named procedure; if it contains the value 2 control will pass to the second-named procedure. If the data item RECORD-TYPE contains a value which does not have a corresponding procedure name following the GO TO (such as 0 or 3 or more in the example), the program will continue in sequence with the statement in the next sentence.

For the GO TO . . . DEPENDING to function correctly, the data name which follows the word DEPENDING must contain a positive or unsigned integer, otherwise the program will continue in its normal sequence.

Read, and sometimes Write, instructions are followed by AT END or INVALID KEY phrases. These are examples of condition tests and may be followed by a GO TO command. For example

    READ CUST-FILE INVALID KEY GO TO MISMATCH.
          ⋮

MISMATCH.   procedures for handling a mismatch on customer file.

There is some controversy in the computer programming world
about the use of GO TO instructions, especially unconditional GO
TOs. Some programmers have noticed that as program become
more complex they tend to have more GO TO statements and these
often lead to an increasing number of logical errors. This has led
them to structure their programs in such a way as to eliminate all, or
virtually all, GO TO statements.

This book is not concerned with the intricacies of programming as
such, and this is not the place to get embroiled in controversy over
the use of the GO TO statement. Clearly it makes sense to structure
programs in as clear and logical a manner as possible, and this may
be achieved through writing the program in a series of modules or
procedures which can be performed as required. But to insist on a
rigid structure that may complicate simple procedures such as
READ . . . AT END so as to eliminate what is, after all, a valid
instruction might well be regarded as an extreme step.

The sequence of operations in a program may be modified even
further through the use of the ALTER statement which alters the
destination of a GO TO instruction. The format is

ALTER procedure-name-1 TO PROCEED TO procedure-
name-2.

where procedure-name-1 is a paragraph consisting of a single GO
TO only.

As an example, suppose a customer file consists of three different
types of record (as in Fig. 7.7), the first type containing customer
name and two lines of address, the second record type containing the
third and fourth lines of address and the telephone number, and the
third type containing sales invoice data. Each customer may have
just one record of types 1 and 2, but any number of records of type 3.
The processing may take the following form:

```
PROCEDURE DIVISION.
    :

READ-CUST-RECORD.
    READ CUST-FILE AT END GO TO FINISH.
ALTER-SWITCH.
    GO TO TYPE-1.
TYPE-1.
    MOVE CUST-NO TO W-CUST-NO.
    MOVE CUST-NAME TO W-CUST-NAME.
    MOVE CUST-ADD-1 TO W-CUST-ADD-1.
```

```
    MOVE CUST-ADD-2 TO W-CUST-ADD-2.
    ALTER ALTER-SWITCH TO PROCEED TO TYPE-2.
    GO TO READ-CUST-RECORD.
TYPE-2.
    MOVE CUST-ADD-3 TO W-CUST-ADD-3.
    MOVE CUST-ADD-4 TO W-CUST-ADD-4.
    ALTER ALTER-SWITCH TO PROCEED TO TYPE-3.
    GO TO READ-CUST-RECORD.
TYPE-3.
    IF CUST-NO NOT = W-CUST-NO GO TO
    END-OF-CUST-PARA.
    :  sales record processing
    .

    GO TO READ-CUST-RECORD.
END-OF-CUST-PARA.
       :  end of customer procedures
       .

    IF EOF-SWITCH = "E" GO TO ENDIT.
    GO TO TYPE-1.
FINISH.
    MOVE "E" TO EOF-SWITCH.
    GO TO END-OF-CUST-PARA.
ENDIT.
    CLOSE CUST-FILE.
    STOP RUN.
```

In this example the GO TO in paragraph ALTER-SWITCH is initially set to direct the program to TYPE-1. So on reading the first record control passes to TYPE-1, which contains an ALTER statement that amends the contents of ALTER-SWITCH so as to pass control to TYPE-2 the next time round. Hence when the second record is read control passes to TYPE-2, which in turn changes the contents of ALTER-SWITCH to redirect control to TYPE-3. After reading the third record control passes to TYPE-3. But the third record may be either a sales record or the type 1 record of another customer. This is tested by comparing the customer number on the most recently read record with that of the last known type 1 record.

If the record just read is a sales record processing continues. But note that ALTER-SWITCH is not changed. And so, on reading the fourth record control will pass again to TYPE-3. On change of customer number there can be a branch to a paragraph which handles procedures to be carried out such as printing totals, etc. before branching back to TYPE-1 to handle the new type 1 customer record.

However, if you feel that you must use the ALTER statement do beware. The possibilities of logical errors cropping up are virtually endless and it would be much safer and wiser to program the procedures without recourse to the ALTER.

Performing out-of-sequence routines

In a program it is sometimes necessary to repeat a set of instruction several times in different parts of a program. For example

```
OPEN INPUT SALES-FILE OUTPUT PRINT-FILE.
MOVE SPACE TO PRINT-LINE.
WRITE PRINT-LINE BEFORE PAGE.
WRITE PRINT-LINE FROM HEADING BEFORE 2.
MOVE SPACE TO PRINT-LINE.
MOVE 2 TO LINE-COUNT.
        .
        .
READ-SALES-RECORD
        .

WRITE PRINT-LINE BEFORE 1.
ADD 1 TO LINE-COUNT.
IF LINE-COUNT < 55 GO TO READ-SALES-RECORD.
MOVE SPACE TO PRINT-LINE.
WRITE PRINT-LINE BEFORE PAGE.
WRITE PRINT-LINE FROM HEADING BEFORE 2.
MOVE SPACE TO PRINT-LINE.
MOVE 2 TO LINE-COUNT.
GO TO READ-SALES-RECORD.
```

In this example a sequence of five lines of coding is repeated. Such repetition is to be avoided on efficiency grounds, not only in terms of actual program writing but also of program storage. Ideally source programs written in COBOL for microcomputers should be stored as compactly as possible. Repetition militates against efficient source program storage. In addition, the compilation process will produce identical object coding each time the sequence of coding is encountered. This can increase compilation time and will make the object program larger than it need be.

The PERFORM statement is used to eliminate such duplication. The coding given above could be rewritten as

```
OPEN INPUT SALES-FILE OUTPUT PRINT-FILE.
PERFORM NEW-PAGE.
        .
        .
READ-SALES-RECORD.
        .
```

```
WRITE PRINT-LINE BEFORE 1.
ADD 1 TO LINE-COUNT.
IF LINE-COUNT > 54 PERFORM NEW-PAGE.
GO TO READ-SALES-RECORD.
      .

NEW-PAGE.
    MOVE SPACE TO PRINT-LINE.
    WRITE PRINT-LINE BEFORE PAGE.
    WRITE PRINT-LINE FROM HEADING BEFORE 2.
    MOVE SPACE TO PRINT-LINE.
    MOVE 2 TO LINE-COUNT.
```

The PERFORM enables the program to go out of sequence temporarily in order to execute some other procedure. After executing the out-of-sequence procedure, control returns to the statement immediately following the PERFORM. In the compilation process, on encountering a procedure to be performed, a dummy, unseen, GO TO is placed at the end of the procedure.

At run time, the PERFORM causes the memory storage address of the statement following the PERFORM to be put into the dummy GO TO. The out-of-sequence procedure is then executed, and the dummy GO TO sends control back to the statement immediately following the PERFORM. Then the dummy GO TO is set to a null (dummy unexecuted) instruction code. This means that if the procedure is executed other than through a PERFORM, processing will continue right through to the next statement as though it were a normal procedure.

The procedure to be executed out of sequence can, in fact, be a series of successive paragraphs or sections, in which case the statement might be written as

PERFORM PARAGRAPH-1 THRU PARAGRAPH-10.

This would send the program out of sequence to PARAGRAPH-1 and will cause the statements in all successive paragraphs, up to and including PARAGRAPH-10, to be executed.

When using the THRU option the second-named procedure must follow the first-named procedure.

The entry in the PERFORM statement may refer to a section name rather than a paragraph name. In this case the out-of-sequence routine will start with the first statement in the first paragraph of the section and will end with the last statement in the last paragraph of the section.

120

A procedure which is being performed may itself contain a PER-FORM instruction. Such a secondary PERFORMed procedure must be wholly inside or wholly outside the primary PERFORMed procedure. Figures 9.1 and 9.2 illustrate correct usage, while Fig. 9.3 and 9.4 illustrate incorrect usage.

Where there are two or more possible exit routes from a procedure or series of procedures, the EXIT statement provides a common exit point. For example

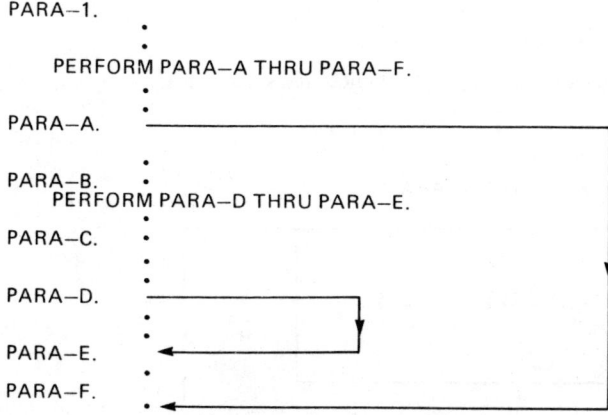

Fig. 9.1 Correct use of a secondary PERFORMed procedure (1)

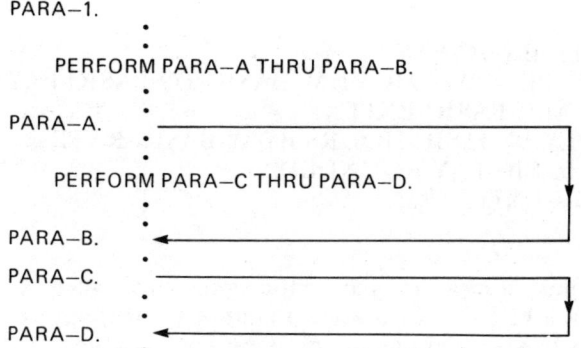

Fig. 9.2 Correct use of a secondary PERFORMed procedure (2)

121

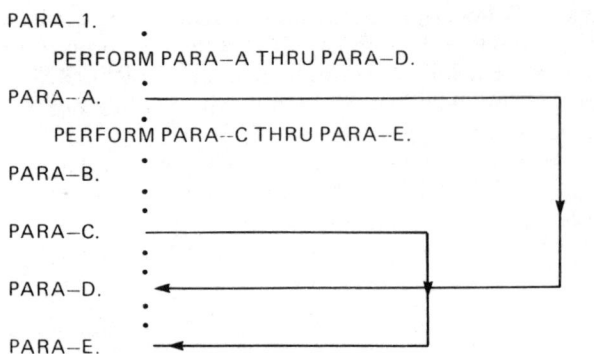

Fig. 9.3 Incorrect use of a secondary PERFORMed procedure (1)

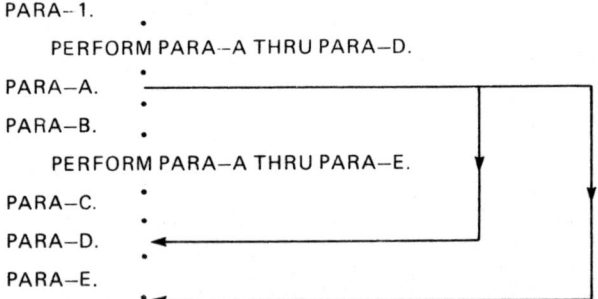

Fig. 9.4 Incorrect use of a secondary PERFORMed procedure (2).

PERFORM CALCULATE-BASIC-PAY THRU
CALC-BASIC-EXIT.

CALCULATE-BASIC-PAY.
IF PAY-TYPE = "W" MOVE W-BASIC TO BASIC-PAY
GO TO CALC-BASIC-EXIT.
MULTIPLY W-BASIC-HOURS BY W-BASIC-RATE
GIVING BASIC-PAY ROUNDED.
CALC-BASIC-EXIT.
EXIT.

The word EXIT must appear in a paragraph as the only sentence.
Another format of PERFORM enables an out-of-sequence procedure to be executed a specified number of times. For example

PERFORM PARA-A 10 TIMES.

will cause the procedure PARA-A to be executed 10 times before continuing in sequence with the statement following the PER-FORM.

It is also possible to use a data item to store the number of times the procedure is to be performed. For example

PERFORM PARA-X CNT TIMES.

In this case a count is set up and the number of times held in the data item is tested when the PERFORM is carried out the first time. The count is then decremented by 1 each time the procedure is executed. When the count equals zero, control returns to the statement following the PERFORM.

If the initial value of the data item used in the PERFORM TIMES is zero or negative the procedure is not executed.

The STOP statement

The execution of the STOP statement causes the program to halt. A

STOP RUN

instruction causes the run-time system to initiate its program ending procedures and then returns control to the operating system.

A temporary halt can be issued through the

STOP literal

command. For example

STOP 1234.

will cause the message 1234 to be displayed at the top left-hand corner of the VDU screen. On pressing carriage return the operator will cause the program to resume with the statement following the STOP. The literal itself may be numeric, non-numeric or a figurative constant (except that ALL must not be used).

Summary

While COBOL program instructions are normally executed in the sequence in which they are written there are ways of changing the sequence of operation permanently or temporarily through the GO TO and PERFORM statements. Both these statements have optional attributes, with the GO TO enabling control to be passed to any one of several possible procedures, and the PERFORM enabling procedures to be executed a number of times.

These sequence changes are normally the result of logical operations or comparisons. The logical operations may be implicit, as in end of file or invalid key conditions in file handling procedures. But, more commonly, the logical operations are controlled explicitly by the IF statement which enables data items to be examined for numeric or alphabetic values; if numeric for being positive, negative or zero; or the contents of two data items may be compared.

Self-test questions

1 When is an IF instruction regarded as a type numeric comparison?

2 A program contains the following sequence of instructions:

```
IF VAL-X NOT < 24 NEXT SENTENCE ELSE
ADD 14 TO VAL-Y
ADD 1 TO TOTAL-1.
DIVIDE 17 INTO VAL-Y GIVING SUB-VAL ROUNDED.
```

What is the instruction executed immediately after the IF when
(a) VAL-X contains the value 4
(b) VAL-X contains 24
(c) VAL-X contains 44.

3 What is wrong with the following sequences of procedures?

```
(a)    PERFORM ADD-LOOP THRU ADD-LOOP-EX.
       :
       ADD-LOOP.
          ADD 1 TO CNT.
          IF CNT < 4 PERFORM ADD-LOOP THRU ADD-
          LOOP-EX.
          MOVE TOTAL (CNT) TO P-TOTAL (CNT).
       ADD-LOOP-EX.
          EXIT.

(b)    PERFORM ADD-LOOP THRU ADD-LOOP-EX.
       :
       ADD-LOOP.
          IF CNT > GO TO ADD-LOOP-EX.
          PERFORM MOVE-TOTAL THRU PRINT-TOTAL.
          MOVE VAL-TOT TO PRINT-TOT.
```

```
MOVE-TOTAL.
    MOVE TOT (CNT) TO P-TOT (CNT).
    ADD TOT (CNT) TO VAL-TOT.
ADD-LOOP-EX.
    EXIT.
PRINT-TOTAL.
    WRITE PRINT-RECORD BEFORE 1.
    ADD 1 TO CNT.
```

4 A statement reads

> GO TO PARA-A PARA-A PARA-X PARA-C PARA-F
> DEPENDING ON VAL-1.

What procedure name will the program pass control to if VAL-1
contains

  (a)   0
  (b)   1
  (c)   3
  (d)   5
  (e)   7

10
Interactive processing

A major advantage of microcomputer COBOL over competing programming languages such as BASIC is the facility of interactive processing by means of pseudo-forms, where the VDU screen is divided into protected areas which can hold text to be displayed on the screen, and permitted areas into which the operator can enter text.

The precise programming methods used will vary from one version of microcomputer COBOL to another. This chapter will look at the approach followed in the version known as CIS COBOL.

The first stage in the use of CIS COBOL is to configure the run-time system, the program which controls the execution of the object programs, for the type of VDU that is being used. This is done by running a utility program called CONFIG.COM which holds information about the characteristics of a number of VDUs. The same utility program is used to configure the FORMS II utility package which is designed to simplify screen pseudo-form creation. Details for configuring particular types of VDU are supplied with the CIS COBOL software and are outside the scope of this chapter which is concerned with the COBOL language coding required for interactive processing.

For VDU screen handling, source program entries are required in the Data and Procedure Divisions, though, additionally, entries may be made in the Environment Division.

Environment Division coding

The Environment Division entry that ought to be used, though it may be omitted, requires that the SPECIAL-NAMES paragraph be used as follows:

```
SPECIAL-NAMES.
    CONSOLE IS CRT.
```

The CONSOLE IS CRT phrase is a CIS COBOL extension to the

language which is designed to enable data to be accepted from or displayed at any position on the VDU screen.

Data Division coding

All data accepted from or displayed on the VDU screen makes use of the Working-Storage Section of the Data Division. Screen data is described like any other, though there are a few special rules that need to be remembered.

1. All data, including numeric values, must be of USAGE DISPLAY, which is the default usage when describing data. This means that USAGE COMP and COMP-3 data items are not allowed. However, edited numeric data items are allowed, and these will be treated as though they were described as alphanumeric.
2. Data can be input to or output from a single data name only. This is often, though not necessarily, a group item.
3. The data item name FILLER has a special meaning in the context of screen handling.

(a) On input of data from the screen, all data items described as FILLER are protected from operator entry into the positions defined by the FILLER entry. For example

```
     01   DATE-HEAD   PIC X(21)   VALUE
               'Enter date ] / / ['.
     01   ENTER-DATE REDEFINES DATE-HEAD.
          02   FILLER            PIC X(12).
          02   ENTER-DAY         PIC 99.
          02   FILLER            PIC X.
          02   ENTER-MONTH       PIC 99.
          02   FILLER            PIC X.
          02   ENTER-YEAR        PIC 99.
          02   FILLER            PIC X.
```

The operator, when asked to enter the date, will find that the first 12 positions of the group data item are protected (i.e. the message 'Enter date]'). Values can be entered into the 13th and 14th screen positions, after which the cursor jumps automatically to the 16th position, bypassing the 15th. This is how the system operates, even though the area of memory storage holding the prompt to the operator and the response from the operator are one and the same.
(b) On sending output to the screen, any data item described as FILLER will cause suppression of the contents of the corresponding

127

area of memory storage. In order to get the prompt displayed in (a) above, it is necessary to display the data item DATA-HEAD which contains no FILLER elementary fields.

Procedure Division coding

The ACCEPT statement is used as the means of inputting data from the VDU screen into memory storage. An example is

ACCEPT ENTER-INPUT.

where ENTER-INPUT is the name of the area in Working-Storage that is to hold the contents of the data transferred from the screen into memory storage. As many characters as specified in the data item ENTER-INPUT will be moved from the top left-hand corner of the screen into memory. The number of characters that may be transferred is limited only by the capacity and characteristics of the VDU screen itself. In most cases this is 1920 characters, with the screen being composed of 24 lines each of 80 characters.

The ACCEPT statement itself halts computer operations and allows the operator to key in the data to be transferred to memory storage. Data can be keyed into those positions on the screen which are considered permitted, that is the screen positions corresponding to the non-FILLER components of the data item. This is controlled by the movement of the cursor which will position itself only against permitted areas.

Consider the program in Fig. 10.1. Lines 007500–008600 define ENTER-INPUT, the area into which the data is to be transferred as a result of the ACCEPT statement. The first 264 character positions are specified as FILLER. This means that the top three lines (of 80 characters) and the first 24 characters positions on the fourth line are protected from operator entry. The cursor will not be positioned in that area; its initial position will be in character position 265 and will permit five characters to be entered, before skipping a further 155 character positions. In other words, when the cursor reaches a position corresponding to a FILLER data item it automatically skips to the start of the next non-FILLER position.

The operator is free to enter data into the permitted areas and to make any amendments to entered data before pressing the carriage return key. To aid data entry, the cursor control keys may be used to position the cursor at the start of a preceding field, the start of the current field, the start of the next field, or one character position backward or one position forward. The setting up of the cursor control keys is part of the configuration function mentioned earlier in this chapter.

```
000100 IDENTIFICATION DIVISION.
000200 PROGRAM-ID.  UPDT.
000300 ENVIRONMENT DIVISION.
000400 CONFIGURATION SECTION.
000500 SOURCE-COMPUTER.   MODEL-XYZ.
000600 OBJECT-COMPUTER.   MODEL-XYZ.
000700 SPECIAL-NAMES.      CONSOLE IS CRT.
000800 INPUT-OUTPUT SECTION.
000900 FILE-CONTROL.
001000      SELECT PRODUCT-FILE ASSIGN TO "PRODUCT.DAT"
001100           ORGANIZATION IS INDEXED
001200           ACCESS MODE IS RANDOM
001300           RECORD KEY IS PRODUCT-NO.
002000 DATA DIVISION.
002100 FILE SECTION.
002200 FD   PRODUCT-FILE.
002300 01   PRODUCT-RECORD.
002400      02   PRODUCT-NO     PIC X(5).
002500      02   PRODUCT-DESC   PIC X(20).
002600      02   PRODUCT-PRICE  PIC 9(4)V99.
002700      02   PRODUCT-QTY    PIC 9(4).
002800      02   PRODUCT-DATE.
002900           03   PRODUCT-YEAR    PIC 99.
003000           03   PRODUCT-MONTH   PIC 99.
003100           03   PRODUCT-DAY     PIC 99.
004000 WORKING-STORAGE SECTION.
004100 77   CHANGE-TAG    PIC 9.
004200 77   INSERT-TAG    PIC 9.
004300 01   W-PRICE       PIC 9(4)V99.
004400 01   W-DATA REDEFINES W-PRICE.
004500      02   W-POUND   PIC 9(4).
004600      02   W-PENCE   PIC 99.
004700 01   NO-TEST.
004800      02   NO-DIG1-2 PIC XX.
004900      02   NO-DIG3-5 PIC 999.
005000 01   HEAD-1  PIC X(38) VALUE
005100      "PROGRAM: UPDT - UPDATE OF PRODUCT FILE".
005200 01   DATE-HEAD      PIC X(21) VALUE "Enter Date ] / / [".
005300 01   ENTER-DATE   REDEFINES  DATE-HEAD.
005400      02   FILLER         PIC X(12).
005500      02   ENTER-DAY      PIC 99.
005600      02   FILLER         PIC X.
005700      02   ENTER-MONTH    PIC 99.
005800      02   FILLER         PIC X.
005900      02   ENTER-YEAR     PIC 99.
006000      02   FILLER         PIC X.
006100 01   INPUT-HEADS.
006200      02   FILLER         PIC X(30).
006300      02   INPUT-HD1      PIC X(19) VALUE "PRODUCT FILE UPDATE".
006400      02   FILLER         PIC X(61).
006500      02   INPUT-HD2      PIC X(19) VALUE "-------------------".
006600      02   FILLER         PIC X(121).
006700      02   INPUT-HD3      PIC X(20) VALUE "PRODUCT NO  ]     [".
006800      02   FILLER         PIC X(140).
006900      02   INPUT-HD4      PIC X(35) VALUE
007000      "DESCRIPTION  ]                    [".
007100      02   FILLER         PIC X(125).
007200      02   INPUT-HD5      PIC X(22) VALUE "PRICE          ]  . [".
007300      02   FILLER         PIC X(138).
007400      02   INPUT-HD6      PIC X(19) VALUE "QUANTITY       ]   [".
007500 01   ENTER-INPUT   REDEFINES  INPUT-HEADS.
007600      02   FILLER         PIC X(264).
007700      02   ENTER-NO       PIC X(5).
007800      02   FILLER         PIC X(155).
007900      02   ENTER-DESC     PIC X(20).
008000      02   FILLER         PIC X(140).
008100      02   ENTER-POUND    PIC 9(4).
008200      02   FILLER         PIC X.
008300      02   ENTER-PENCE    PIC 99.
```

```
008400      02  FILLER        PIC X(153).
008500      02  ENTER-QTY     PIC 9(4).
008600      02  FILLER        PIC X.
008700  01  HOLD-SCREEN       PIC X(749).
010000  PROCEDURE DIVISION.
010100*
010200*  CLEAR SCREEN, ENTER HEADING THEN ENTER DATE
010300*       AND CHECK DATE FOR VALIDITY
010400*
010500  HEAD-DISPLAY.
010600      DISPLAY SPACE.
010700      DISPLAY HEAD-1 AT 0122.
010800      DISPLAY DATE-HEAD AT 0301.
010900  DATE-ENTRY.
011000      ACCEPT ENTER-DATE AT 0301.
011100      IF ENTER-YEAR < 00 GO TO BAD-DATE.
011200      IF ENTER-YEAR > 85 GO TO BAD-DATE.
011400      IF ENTER-DAY < 01 GO TO BAD-DATE.
011500      IF ENTER-DAY > 31 GO TO BAD-DATE.
011600      IF ENTER-MONTH < 01 GO TO BAD-DATE.
011700      IF ENTER-MONTH > 12 GO TO BAD-DATE.
011800      GO TO MAIN-DISPLAY.
011900  BAD-DATE.
012000      DISPLAY "** INVALID DATE **" AT 0632.
012100      GO TO DATE-ENTRY.
012200*
012300*  CLEAR SCREEN, DISPLAY INPUT HEADINGS & OPEN PRODUCTS FILE
012400*
020000  MAIN-DISPLAY.
020100      DISPLAY SPACE.
020200      DISPLAY INPUT-HEADS.
020300      OPEN I-O PRODUCT-FILE.
020400*
020500*  MAIN LOOP -- Accept input, Check validity of product no.
020600*              if valid, read record and display contents
020700*              if no record, then insertion
020800*
020900  INPUT-DATA.
021000      MOVE SPACE TO ENTER-INPUT.
021050      DISPLAY ENTER-INPUT.
021100      DISPLAY "                              " AT 1501.
021200      ACCEPT ENTER-INPUT.
021300      IF ENTER-NO = "END" GO TO FINISH.
021400      MOVE ENTER-NO TO NO-TEST.
021500      IF NO-DIG1-2 < "AA" GO TO BAD-NO.
021550      IF NO-DIG1-2 > "ZZ" GO TO BAD-NO.
021600      IF NO-DIG1-2 = SPACE GO TO BAD-NO.
021700      IF NO-DIG3-5 < 000 GO TO BAD-NO.
021750      IF NO-DIG3-5 > 999 GO TO BAD-NO.
021800      MOVE ENTER-NO TO PRODUCT-NO.
021900      READ PRODUCT-FILE INVALID KEY GO TO INSERTION.
022000      MOVE 0 TO INSERT-TAG.
022100      MOVE PRODUCT-DESC TO ENTER-DESC.
022200      MOVE PRODUCT-PRICE TO W-PRICE.
022300      MOVE W-POUND TO ENTER-POUND.
022400      MOVE W-PENCE TO ENTER-PENCE.
022500      MOVE PRODUCT-QTY TO ENTER-QTY.
022600      DISPLAY ENTER-INPUT.
022700      MOVE ENTER-INPUT TO HOLD-SCREEN.
022800  ACCEPT-CHANGE.
022900      ACCEPT ENTER-INPUT.
023000      IF ENTER-NO = NO-TEST GO TO UPDATE-FILE.
023100*
023200*  Update data entered for a different product no. - error
023300*
023400      MOVE HOLD-SCREEN TO ENTER-INPUT.
023500      DISPLAY ENTER-INPUT.
023600      DISPLAY "* LAST DATA ENTERED IS FOR DIFFERENT PRODUCT *"
023700          AT 1501.
```

130

```
023800      GO TO ACCEPT-CHANGE.
023900*
024000 BAD-NO.
024100      DISPLAY "* INVALID PRODUCT NO. *" AT 1501.
024200      GO TO INPUT-DATA.
030000*
030100*   Validate Input
030200*
030300 UPDATE-FILE.
030400      IF ENTER-POUND NOT NUMERIC GO TO BAD-VALUE.
030500      IF ENTER-PENCE NOT NUMERIC GO TO BAD-VALUE.
030600      IF ENTER-QTY NOT NUMERIC GO TO BAD-QTY.
030700      MOVE 0 TO CHANGE-TAG.
030800      IF ENTER-DESC = PRODUCT-DESC GO TO UPDATE-POUND.
030900      MOVE ENTER-DESC TO PRODUCT-DESC.
031000      MOVE 1 TO CHANGE-TAG.
031100 UPDATE-POUND.
031200      IF ENTER-POUND = W-POUND GO TO UPDATE-PENCE.
031300      MOVE ENTER-POUND TO W-POUND.
031400      MOVE 1 TO CHANGE-TAG.
031500 UPDATE-PENCE.
031600      IF ENTER-PENCE = W-PENCE GO TO UPDATE-VAL.
031700      MOVE ENTER-PENCE TO W-PENCE.
031800      MOVE 1 TO CHANGE-TAG.
031900 UPDATE-VAL.
032000      IF CHANGE-TAG = 0 GO TO UPDATE-QTY.
032100      MOVE W-PRICE TO PRODUCT-PRICE.
032200 UPDATE-QTY.
032300      IF ENTER-QTY = PRODUCT-QTY GO TO TEST-CHANGE-TAG.
032400      MOVE ENTER-QTY TO PRODUCT-QTY.
032500      MOVE 1 TO CHANGE-TAG.
032600 TEST-CHANGE-TAG.
032700      IF CHANGE-TAG = 0 GO TO INPUT-DATA.
032800      MOVE ENTER-DAY TO PRODUCT-DAY.
032900      MOVE ENTER-MONTH TO PRODUCT-MONTH.
033000      MOVE ENTER-YEAR TO PRODUCT-YEAR.
033100      IF INSERT-TAG = 0 GO TO REWRITE-RECORD.
033200      WRITE PRODUCT-RECORD INVALID KEY GO TO INPUT-DATA.
033300      GO TO INPUT-DATA.
033400 REWRITE-RECORD.
033500      REWRITE PRODUCT-RECORD INVALID GO TO INPUT-DATA.
033600      GO TO INPUT-DATA.
040000*
040100*      Insert - set tag to 1, set up record
040200*
040300 INSERTION.
040400      MOVE 1 TO INSERT-TAG.
040500      MOVE SPACE TO PRODUCT-RECORD.
040600      MOVE ENTER-NO TO PRODUCT-NO.
040700      GO TO ACCEPT-CHANGE.
040800*
040900 BAD-VALUE.
041000      DISPLAY "* INVALID PRICE *" AT 1501.
041100      GO TO ACCEPT-CHANGE.
041200 BAD-QTY.
041300      DISPLAY "* INVALID QUANTITY *" AT 1501.
041400      GO TO ACCEPT-CHANGE.
050000 FINISH.
050100      CLOSE PRODUCT-FILE.
050200      DISPLAY SPACE.
050300      DISPLAY "END OF PRODUCT FILE UPDATE" AT 0128.
050400      STOP RUN.
```

Fig. 10.1

On entering data at the keyboard, if the data item being filled is defined as PICTURE X any character may be keyed into the current cursor position. But if the data item is defined as PICTURE 9 only numerals may be entered; the entry of a decimal point will cause leading zeros to be automatically entered into the field; an attempt to enter any other character into a PICTURE 9 field will fail, through the entry not being activated—it is as though the key had not been depressed.

Operator entry ceases on pressing the carriage return key whereupon control passes to the next statement in the program following the ACCEPT.

While the ACCEPT normally starts from the first cursor position on the VDU screen (top left-hand corner), it may be specified to accept data starting at any other position. For example

ACCEPT ENTER-DATE AT 0301.

The number following the word AT is a four-digit number. The first two digits denote the line number on the screen where entry is to start, 01 being the first line number. The last two digits denote the character position on the line, 01 being the first character position. Thus 0301 means that the entry is to start at the first position on the third line.

It is acceptable to have an entry which reads

ACCEPT ENTER-VALUE AT SCREEN-POSITION.

provided that SCREEN-POSITION is defined as a four-digit numeric data item, and that its contents follow the rules for specifying the VDU screen address in terms of line number and character position number as given in the last paragraph.

The DISPLAY statement is used to transfer data from memory storage to the VDU screen. The format of the statement is

DISPLAY INPUT-HEADS.

This tells the program to transfer the contents of the data item called INPUT-HEADS to the VDU, starting at line 01 character position 01. Any number of characters may be sent, up to the maximum number that can be accommodated on a VDU screen, normally 1920.

Looking at the program (Fig. 10.1), INPUT-HEADS is described as a group item in lines 006100–007400. Where an elementary constituent item is defined as FILLER, the corresponding position on the screen is set to spaces. The overall effect of the display is to create a screen which looks like Fig. 10.2. This is an example of a pseudo-form which can be completed by means of an ACCEPT statement to look like Fig. 10.3.

As in the case of the ACCEPT statement, it is possible to specify where on the VDU screen data is to be displayed. For example we could write

DISPLAY DATE-HEAD AT 0301.

This would cause the data item to be displayed on the VDU screen

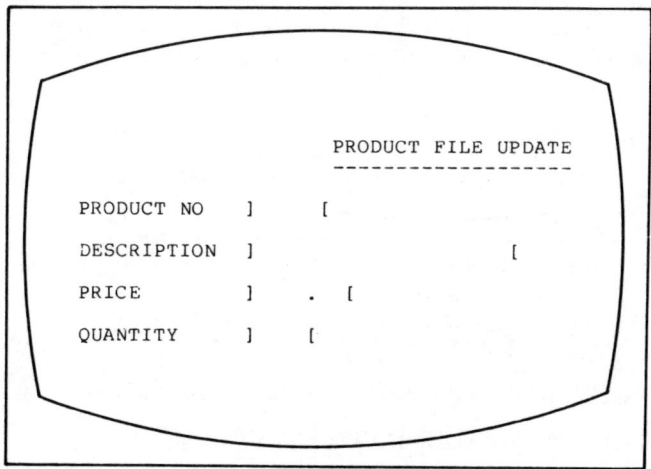

Fig. 10.2

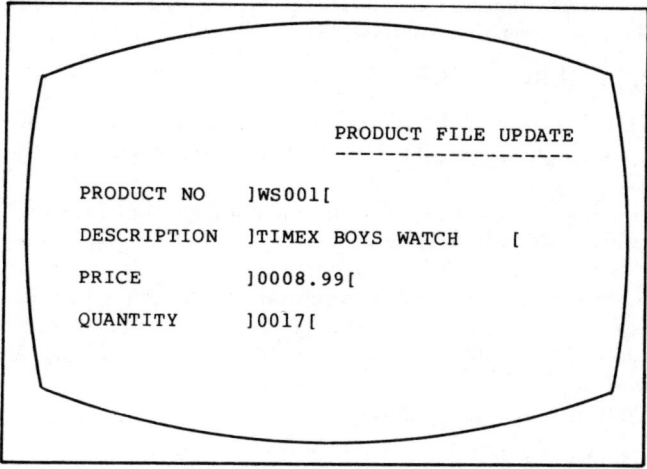

Fig. 10.3

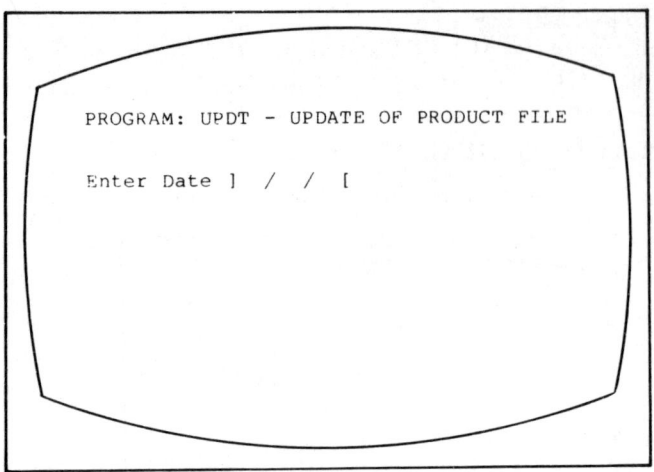

Fig. 10.4

starting at the first character position on the third line as in Fig. 10.4.

The data which is being displayed may be a literal. For example

DISPLAY "** INVALID DATE **" AT 0632.

or

DISPLAY 152 at 0120.

If a figurative constant is specified as the data to be displayed, only a single occurrence is in fact displayed. So

DISPLAY ZERO AT 0201.

will cause a single zero to be displayed on the second line of the VDU screen at the first position. However, the instruction

DISPLAY SPACE.

will cause the entire VDU screen to be cleared by filling it with spaces.

Figure 10.1 is an example of an interactive program which can insert new and amend existing product records. The initial screen procedures are, first of all, to clear the screen and then display the program heading.

Line 010800 displays the prompt

Enter Date] / / [

starting in line 3 character position 1, and this is followed in line

134

011000 by an instruction to accept the date. The cursor will allow numerals only to be entered into the blank positions between the field boundary markers. The program then checks for a valid date. If the entered date is valid processing of input is allowed; if the date is invalid an error message is displayed and control passes to the ACCEPT statement to enable the operator to re-enter the date.

A point to note is that the date prompt, DATE-HEAD, and the area into which the date is entered, ENTER-DATE, occupy the same memory storage positions, with ENTER-DATE being a redefinition of DATE-HEAD. The use of FILLER at the elementary data item level ensures that the day, month and year are put into their correct positions.

The main pseudo-form is described in lines 006100–008600, the actual data being entered into the group item ENTER-INPUT, which is a redefinition of the form entry INPUT-HEADS. The procedures initially clear the screen to space and then display the headings-only part of the pseudo-form (lines 021000–021050).

For each form's worth of data entered, the data area in Working-Storage, ENTER-INPUT, is cleared to spaces, as is the error message line on the screen, and the program pauses to allow the operator to enter the data. If the product code entered is 'END', control of the program is passed to the end routine (lines 050000–050400), otherwise the product code is checked for validity. If the code is invalid, an error message is displayed and control returns to the ACCEPT statement which allows the operator to re-enter the data.

Valid data updates the product file before clearing the data area of the pseudo-form in preparation for the next input data.

The definition of forms requires care to ensure that the FILLER entries are in the right place so as to ensure that the data is entered into the required character positions on the screen. An error will lead, at best, to a messy and confusing display. For example, suppose line 005400 of the program had been entered as

    02   FILLER   PIC X(2).

by mistake. The ACCEPT would then start by moving the cursor the third character instead of the thirteenth, and the entry of the date 5th January 1983 would show the screen with the line looking like

    En05r01a83] / /[

although the date itself would be in the correct elementary data fields and would be usable.

The FORMS II utility program

The creation of large, complex pseudo-forms gives plenty of scope for errors to be made. To facilitate the creation of forms for their CIS COBOL system, Microfocus has developed a utility program called FORMS II.

At its simplest level FORMS II allows the programmer to experiment with possible pseudo-form layouts for data entry before creating the final version. The pseudo-form headings are entered first as fixed text on a blank screen. After this fixed text portion is created, it is displayed on the screen as a background to enable the data descriptions to be entered in their correct positions as variable data. The variable data entries may be alphanumeric or numeric, and if numeric may include numeric editing symbols.

FORMS II creates a record on disc with a suffix .DDS which contains the generated data description statement. This is in a form which can be copied directly into the Working-Storage Section of a COBOL program. Figure 10.5 is an example of a .DDS file created by FORMS II.

The data description statements generated by FORMS II usually occupy more lines of coding, and therefore require more source program file storage space on disc, than most efficient programmer-defined data descriptions. The programmer may amend the FORMS II generated data descriptions in order to save space.

FORMS II can also generate a program to enable the user to check that the generated data description coding works correctly. When the program is run, it displays the pseudo-form and allows data to be entered into the various fields to check out the form.

The utility program can even generate a usable program for the

```
B>TYPE CLUB.DDS
     01    CLUB-00    .
           03 FILLER              PIC X(0024).
           03   CLUB-00-0001      PIC X(0015) VALUE "XYZ SPORTS CLUB".
           03 FILLER              PIC X(0228).
           03   CLUB-00-0002      PIC X(0009) VALUE "MAIN MENU".
           03 FILLER              PIC X(0212).
           03   CLUB-00-0003      PIC X(0019) VALUE "1 = MEMBER BOOKINGS".
           03 FILLER              PIC X(0141).
           03   CLUB-00-0004      PIC X(0017) VALUE "2 = CLUB BOOKINGS".
           03 FILLER              PIC X(0143).
           03   CLUB-00-0005      PIC X(0012) VALUE "3 = PAYMENTS".
           03 FILLER              PIC X(0308).
           03   CLUB-00-0006      PIC X(0012) VALUE "ENTER OPTION".
           03 FILLER              PIC X(0004).
           03   CLUB-00-0007      PIC X(0003) VALUE "] [".
     01    CLUB-01      REDEFINES    CLUB-00    .
           03 FILLER              PIC X(1145).
           03   CLUB-01-0001      PIC 9(0001).
```

Fig. 10.5 Example of a file created by the FORMS II utility program

136

creation and maintenance of an indexed file. During the stage when the variable data is described, the record key is specified. FORMS II then generates the necessary coding to create a full program that enables new records to be inserted into the file and existing records amended or deleted. The generated program can also access records for viewing randomly or sequentially. However, the program does have its limitations, the file record being limited to the fields described on the pseudo-form. It also lacks many of the types of validation of input which are commonly used, such as range tests and check-digit verification.

Summary

Interactive processing is regarded as a simple data processing function where data can be transferred between the operator and the Working-Storage Section of the program through pseudo-forms on a VDU screen. The conventional COBOL statements of ACCEPT and DISPLAY are used for this type of data transfer, with all the data being in character (or USAGE DISPLAY) mode.

While different versions of microcomputer COBOL handle interactive processing in slightly different ways, the method explained was the approach used in the popular CIS COBOL whose producers have also created a useful forms creation utility program called FORMS II.

Self-test questions

1 What Procedure Division statements are used to pass data between the program and the VDU screen?

2 A data entry is described as follows:

```
01  SCREEN-HEADINGS.
    02  ENTRY-1  PIC X(21) VALUE
        "SUPPLIER CODE ] [".
    02  FILLER    PIC X(59).
    02  ENTRY-2  PIC X(16) VALUE
        "SUPPLIER NAME ]".
    02  FILLER    PIC X(20).
    02  ENTRY-3  PIC X VALUE "[".
01  DATA-INPUT REDEFINES SCREEN-HEADINGS.
```

Complete the data description entry so as to enable the operator to enter data into the correct permitted areas.

137

3 Assuming that the data entry described in question 2 is correctly entered in the source program, into which character position on which line will the operator begin to enter the supplier name?

4 Using the .DDS file as described in Fig. 10.5, show the skeleton screen layout.

11
Table handling

In describing the methods of structuring data in Chapter 6 mention was made of the possibility of constructing tables of data through the OCCURS clause. For example, a record description might be

    01 SALES-RECORD.
        02 PRODUCT-NO   PIC X(4).
        02 MONTHS-SALES   PIC   9(6)   OCCURS   12
            TIMES.

This would result in an area of memory storage being reserved for the record which would look like Fig. 11.1.

PROD CODE	MONTH 1 SALES	MONTH 2 SALES	MONTH 3 SALES	MONTH 4 SALES	MONTH 5 SALES	MONTH 6 SALES	MONTH 7 SALES	MONTH 8 SALES	MONTH 9 SALES	MONTH 10 SALES	MONTH 11 SALES	MONTH 12 SALES
4	6	6	6	6	6	6	6	6	6	6	6	6

Fig. 11.1

In other words, the record area contains a table of 12 successive similarly sized data items. In order to retrieve the contents of any of the entries in the table a pointer must be used. This pointer is either a subscript or an index. A table may be handled by either type of pointer, but not both.

Table handling with subscripts

A subscript may be an integer or a data item described in the Data Division which contains an acceptable value. Thus, if the table is described as

    MONTHS-SALES   PIC 9(6) OCCURS 12 TIMES.

an instruction

ADD MONTHS-SALES (1) TO TOTAL-SALES.

is valid and so is

ADD MONTHS-SALES (SUBS) TO TOTAL-SALES.

provided that SUBS is defined as a numeric data item and contains an integer value between 1 and 12. But

ADD MONTHS-SALES (0) TO TOTAL-SALES.

is illegal.

Suppose it is required that each of the twelve entries in the table are to be summed and the sum put into TOTAL-SALES. One method would be to write laboriously

```
ADD MONTHS-SALES (1) MONTH-SALES (2)
    MONTH-SALES (3) MONTH-SALES (4)
    MONTH-SALES (5) MONTH-SALES (6)
    MONTH-SALES (7) MONTH-SALES (8)
    MONTH-SALES (9) MONTH-SALES (10)
    MONTH-SALES (11) MONTH-SALES (12) GIVING
    TOTAL-SALES.
```

Or, alternatively,

```
ADD MONTHS-SALES (1) TO TOTAL-SALES.
ADD MONTHS-SALES (2) TO TOTAL-SALES.
            .
            .
ADD MONTHS-SALES (12) TO TOTAL-SALES.
```

Another method is to add the contents of the table in a loop as follows:

```
01   SUBS   PIC 99 VALUE ZERO.
             .
             .
     MOVE ZERO TO TOTAL-SALES.
ADD-SUBS.
     ADD 1 TO SUBS.
     ADD MONTHS-SALES (SUBS) TO TOTAL-SALES.
     IF SUBS = 12 GO TO CLEAR-SUBS.
     GO TO ADD-SUBS.
CLEAR-SUBS.
     MOVE ZERO TO SUBS.
             .
             .
```

In this example the value of the subscript (SUBS) is initially set to zero. The loop consists of incrementing the subscript by 1 and adding the value stored in the contents of the current position in the table to the total. After the twelfth such addition the subscript will contain 12, which is the number of entries in the table, and the program control will exit from the loop and set the subscript to zero in readiness for further use.

This loop and its associated coding does not reduce the amount of source program coding by very much and so offers little advantage over a series of successive ADD instructions, let along a single ADD instruction with a list of twelve data items before the GIVING. So the problem is how to construct a loop which minimises the amount of source language coding. In Chapter 9 we looked at the use of the PERFORM statement, which allows the program to branch out of normal sequence in order to perform certain procedures before returning control to the statement following the PERFORM.

The summing of the contents of the table MONTHS-SALES can be treated as an out-of-sequence routine. For example

```
01   SUBS   PIC 99   VALUE ZERO.
         .
         .
     PERFORM ADD-SALES 12 TIMES.
     MOVE ZERO TO SUBS.
         .
ADD-SALES.
     ADD 1 TO SUBS.
     ADD MONTHS-SALES (SUBS) TO SALES-TOTAL.
```

In this example, control goes to the out-of-sequence paragraph ADD-SALES 12 times. On each occasion the subscript is incremented by 1 and the contents of the appropriate table entry are added to the total.

Another way of achieving the same effect is to PERFORM until a condition is satisfied. The coding we can use is largely the same as in the previous example except that the PERFORM is written

```
     PERFORM ADD-SALES UNTIL SUBS = 12.
```

These PERFORM options are generally available in all versions of microcomputer COBOL. There is an even more powerful format which is available in some versions, though not in CIS COBOL. This is the PERFORM . . . VARYING format. The summing of the twelve table entries could be rewritten using this format as

```
01   SUBS   PIC 99.
         .
         .
     PERFORM ADD-SALES VARYING SUBS FROM 1
     BY 1 UNTIL SUBS GREATER 12.
         .
         .
```

ADD-SALES.
    ADD MONTHS-SALES (SUBS) TO SALES-TOTAL.

In this version of the PERFORM statement there is no need to initialise the subscript nor is there a need to increment its value. All the subscript handling is controlled by the PERFORM itself.

When the PERFORM is first entered control is under the word FROM. In this case FROM 1 sets the initial value of the subscript SUBS to 1. The system then compares the current value of SUBS (currently 1) against the control value 12. If the current value is not greater than 12, the procedure ADD-SALES is performed.

After performing the out-of-sequence procedure, control passes to the word BY. The expression BY 1 tells the system to increment the value of SUBS by the value 1. And again the current value of SUBS is compared with the control value 12.

After the twelfth time ADD-SALES is performed, control passes to BY and SUBS is incremented by 1 so that it contains the value 13. At this stage the condition test is satisfied, that is SUBS is greater than 12, and the program continues with the statement following the PERFORM.

Great care should be taken when using the PERFORM . . . VARYING statement to ensure that the procedure is executed the required number of times. Remember that the condition is tested after the value of the subscript is incremented. To perform a procedure 12 times therefore requires a test of greater than 12 or equal to 13.

Two- and three-dimensional tables

COBOL permits tables of up to three dimensions. For example, a table may be held in memory defined as follows:

```
01  TABLE-OF-PAY-RATES.
    02  FACTORY   OCCURS 4.
        03  JOB-CODE   OCCURS 10.
            04  RATE    PIC 99V99   OCCURS 3.
```

This would be stored in memory as shown in Fig.11.2.

Any reference to FACTORY will require the use of a subscript containing a value between 1 and 4. Any reference to JOB-CODE will require two subscripts, the first referring to FACTORY and the second to the specific JOB-CODE. If reference is made to RATE three subscripts will be required, the first two as for reference to JOB-CODE and the third to the specific rate within that job code. Thus a reference may be made to FACTORY (SUBS-F) in which

JOB-CODE 1	JOB-CODE 2	JOB-CODE 3	JOB-CODE 4	JOB-CODE 5	JOB-CODE 6	JOB-CODE 7	JOB-CODE 8	JOB-CODE 9	JOB-CODE 10

RATE

JOB-CODE 1	JOB-CODE 2	JOB-CODE 3	JOB-CODE 4	JOB-CODE 5	JOB-CODE 6	JOB-CODE 7	JOB-CODE 8	JOB-CODE 9	JOB-CODE 10

JOB-CODE 1	JOB-CODE 2	JOB-CODE 3	JOB-CODE 4	JOB-CODE 5	JOB-CODE 6	JOB-CODE 7	JOB-CODE 8	JOB-CODE 9	JOB-CODE 10

JOB-CODE 1	JOB-CODE 2	JOB-CODE 3	JOB-CODE 4	JOB-CODE 5	JOB-CODE 6	JOB-CODE 7	JOB-CODE 8	JOB-CODE 9	JOB-CODE 10

Fig. 11.2

143

case the reference is to all the job codes and rates which make up that occurrence of FACTORY.

A reference to an entry within JOB-CODE (SUBS-F, SUBS-J) and a reference to RATE would be written with three subscripts in parentheses, such as

RATE (SUBS-F, SUBS-J, SUBS-R).

The power of the PERFORM . . . VARYING can be demonstrated further by reference to the TABLE-OF-PAY-RATES, the three-dimensional table mentioned above. Suppose each of the rates of pay (written as 04 RATE PIC 99V99 OCCURS 3 TIMES) is to be increased by 10 per cent, the whole procedure could be controlled by a single PERFORM statement such as

```
PERFORM ADD-10PERCENT VARYING SUBS-F FROM
  1 BY 1 UNTIL
  SUBS-F > 4 AFTER VARYING SUBS-J FROM 1 BY 1
  UNTIL
  SUBS-J > 10 AFTER VARYING SUBS-R FROM 1 BY 1
  UNTIL
  SUBS-R > 3.
```

```
ADD-10PERCENT.
  MULTIPLY 1.1 BY RATE (SUBS-F, SUBS-J, SUBS-R)
  ROUNDED.
```

But do remember that while some versions of microcomputer COBOL, such as that for the Tandy TRS-80, have this format of PERFORM, other versions of the language do not. Users of versions lacking this format would have to do the coding in some other, long-handed form.

Table handling with indexing

Where a subscript may be a data item which could be used for several purposes in a program, an index name must be a unique word within the program and cannot be used for any purpose other than indexing.

The index name is first encountered in the OCCURS clause. For example

```
01  SALES-RECORD.
    02  PRODUCT-NO  PIC X(5).
```

```
02   MONTHS-SALES   PIC 9(6) OCCURS 12 TIMES
     INDEXED BY IND.
```

In this example IND is used as the index name, and must be used if an entry in MONTH-SALES is referred to by indexing. Note, however, that an entry in the table can still be referenced by a literal. For example MONTHS-SALES (4) is acceptable as a reference to the fourth entry in the table.

The index name cannot be used to index another table, that is each table which is indexed must have its own unique index name.

Before being used in any table references the index name must be initialised by means of the SET instruction. For example

```
SET IND TO 1.
```

This sets the value of the index name IND to 1. The initial value must be within the possible range of values for that table as specified in the OCCURS statement.

The value of an index name may be modified by a SET instruction. For example

```
SET IND UP BY 2.
```

or

```
SET IND DOWN BY 1.
```

Using the type of coding as shown by subscripts, to sum the contents of MONTHS-SALES round a loop would involve coding such as

```
MOVE ZERO TO TOTAL-SALES.
SET IND TO 1.
ADD-SALES.
ADD MONTHS-SALES (IND) TO TOTAL-SALES.
IF IND = 12 GO TO NEXT-PARA.
SET IND UP BY 1.
GO TO ADD-SALES.
NEXT-PARA.
    :
```

Other than the SET statement, only the PERFORM may modify an index name. Thus instructions like

```
PERFORM ADD-SALES UNTIL IND = 12.
```

or

```
PERFORM ADD-SALES VARYING IND FROM 1 BY 1
    UNTIL IND > 12.
```

are allowed.

A data item may be set up in Working-Storage with the USAGE INDEX such as

    01   INDEX-DATA-ITEM USAGE INDEX.

to be used to hold the setting of an index name, perhaps temporarily, while the index name has its value changed in the execution of a procedure. The program in Fig. 11.3 uses this device.

A useful feature of indexing which subscripting lacks is the facility of relative indexing. For example, a sales analysis may be of sales by colour code within product code within product type within customer within area. Thus there are five levels of analysis. Sub-totals are to be printed on change of any of the five elements listed as well as a grand total at the end. This means that on change of colour code the total sales by that colour code are printed, the sub-total for that colour code is added to the sub-total for the product code, and then the sub-total for the colour code is set to zero in readiness for the next colour code. Similarly, on change of product code the sub-total for the product code is printed and then added to the sub-total for the product type before being set to zero for the new product code data, and so on. We might use entries such as:

    01   TOTALS.
        02   SALES-TOTS   OCCURS 6   INDEXED BY IND.
            03   SALES-VAL   PIC S9(6)V99.
            03   SALES-QTY   PIC S9(8).
                  :

        SET IND TO 1.

        ADD INPUT-VAL TO SALES-VAL (IND).
        ADD INPUT-QTY TO SALES-QTY (IND.)

   INC.-TOTS.
        ADD SALES-VAL (IND) TO SALES-VAL (IND + 1).
        ADD SALES-QTY (IND) TO SALES-QTY (IND + 1).
        MOVE +0 TO SALES-VAL (IND) SALES-QTY (IND).
                  :

        PERFORM INC-TOTS.
                  :

        SET IND TO 3.
                   :

        etc.

In the example, if IND contains the value 1, then IND + 1 will reference the second entry in the table, and so on.

```
01   MLETTERS    PIC X(36) VALUE
     "JANFEBMARAPRMAYJUNJLYAUGSEPOCTNOVDEC".

01   MNAMEX  REDEFINES  MLETTERS.
     02  MNAMES    PIC XXX   OCCURS 12   INDEXED BY IND-M.

01   INDEX-DATA-ITEM   USAGE INDEX.

01   DAYS-IN-MONTH   PIC X(24) VALUE
     "312831303130313130313031".

01   DAYS-IN-M   REDEFINES   DAYS-IN-MONTH.
     02  DAYS-MONTH   PIC 99   OCCURS 12   INDEXED BY IND-D.

01   TOT-DAYS    PIC 999 VALUE ZERO.

01   MONTH-HD    PIC X(19) VALUE "Enter Month No ]   [".

01   ENTER-MONTH   REDEFINES   MONTH-HD.
     02   FILLER    PIC X(16).
     02   THIS-MONTH  PIC 99.

01   DISPLAY-MONTH-NAME.
     02   DISP-1  PIC X(14) VALUE "THIS MONTH IS ".
     02   DISP-2  PIC XXX.

01   DISP-CUM-DAYS.
     02   DISP-3  PIC X(35) VALUE
     "TOTAL DAYS UP TO END OF THIS MONTH".
     02   DISP-4  PIC Z99.

PROCEDURE DIVISION.
              .
              .
     DISPLAY SPACE.
     DISPLAY MONTH-HD AT 0201.

ACCEPT-MONTH.
     ACCEPT ENTER-MONTH AT 0201.
     IF THIS-MONTH < 01 GO TO ACCEPT-MONTH.
     IF THIS-MONTH > 12 GO TO ACCEPT-MONTH.
     SET IND-M TO THIS-MONTH.
     MOVE MNAMES (IND-M) TO DISP-2.
     DISPLAY DISPLAY-MONTH-NAME AT 0301.
     SET INDEX-DATA-ITEM TO IND-M.
     SET IND-D TO 1.
     PERFORM ADD-DAYS UNTIL IND-D > INDEX-DATA-ITEM.
     MOVE TOT-DAYS TO DISP-4.
     DISPLAY DISP-CUM-DAYS.
              .
              .
ADD-DAYS.
     ADD DAYS-MONTH (IND-D) TO TOT-DAYS.
     SET IND-D UP BY 1.
```

Fig. 11.3

Table searching

In the examples of table handling given so far the tables have consisted of perhaps a dozen or so entries. Reference to any of the entries in a small table is easily handled and quickly processed by the methods described.

But suppose a table has over a hundred entries. Finding a particular entry may require little coding but take a disproportionately large amount of processing time, sufficient to be noticeable, particularly if the table is not stored in key sequence. for example, suppose the table consists of a series of entries each being a country code, country name and capital city name. This may be coded as shown in Fig. 11.4, where the list is not in country-code sequence. If it is

COUNTRY LIST IN ALPHABETIC SEQUENCE

```
02   FILLER PIC X(29) VALUE "E30ALBANIA        TIRANA        ".
02   FILLER PIC X(29) VALUE "A13AFGHANISTAN    KABUL         ".
02   FILLER PIC X(29) VALUE "F16ALGERIA        ALGIERS       ".
02   FILLER PIC X(29) VALUE "F29ANGOLA         LUANDA        ".
02   FILLER PIC X(29) VALUE "N24ARGENTINA      BUENOS AIRES  ".
02   FILLER PIC X(29) VALUE "S01AUSTRALIA      CANBERRA      ".
02   FILLER PIC X(29) VALUE "E21AUSTRIA        VIENNA        ".
02   FILLER PIC X(29) VALUE "A17BANGLADESH     DACCA         ".
02   FILLER PIC X(29) VALUE "E07BELGIUM        BRUSSELLS     ".
02   FILLER PIC X(29) VALUE "N04BELIZE         BELMOPAN      ".
02   FILLER PIC X(29) VALUE "F12BENIN          PORTO NOVO    ".
02   FILLER PIC X(29) VALUE "A29BHUTAN         THIMPHU       ".
02   FILLER PIC X(29) VALUE "N23BOLIVIA        LA PAZ        ".
02   FILLER PIC X(29) VALUE "N19BRAZIL         BRASILIA      ".
02   FILLER PIC X(29) VALUE "A25BURMA          RANGOON       ".
02   FILLER PIC X(29) VALUE "F28CAMEROON       YAOUNDE       ".
02   FILLER PIC X(29) VALUE "N02CANADA         OTTAWA        ".
02   FILLER PIC X(29) VALUE "F20CENT AFR REP.BANGUI         ".
02   FILLER PIC X(29) VALUE "F15CHAD           N'DJAMENA     ".
02   FILLER PIC X(29) VALUE "N25CHILE          SANTIAGO      ".
02   FILLER PIC X(29) VALUE "A18CHINA          PEKING        ".
02   FILLER PIC X(29) VALUE "N16COLUMBIA       BOGOTA        ".
02   FILLER PIC X(29) VALUE "F26CONGO          BRAZZAVILLE   ".
02   FILLER PIC X(29) VALUE "N09COSTA RICA     SAN JOSE      ".
02   FILLER PIC X(29) VALUE "A02CYPRUS         NICOSIA       ".
02   FILLER PIC X(29) VALUE "E26CZECHOSLOVAK.PRAGUE         ".
02   FILLER PIC X(29) VALUE "E12DENMARK        COPENHAGEN    ".
02   FILLER PIC X(29) VALUE "N13DOMINICAN REPDOMINICA       ".
02   FILLER PIC X(29) VALUE "E24EAST GERMANY BERLIN         ".
02   FILLER PIC X(29) VALUE "F18EGYPT          CAIRO         ".
02   FILLER PIC X(29) VALUE "E05EIRE           DUBLIN        ".
02   FILLER PIC X(29) VALUE "N06EL SALVADOR    SAN SALVADOR  ".
02   FILLER PIC X(29) VALUE "E01ENGLAND        LONDON        ".
02   FILLER PIC X(29) VALUE "N17EQUADOR        QUITO         ".
02   FILLER PIC X(29) VALUE "F21ETHIOPIA       ADDIS ABABA   ".
02   FILLER PIC X(29) VALUE "S04FIJI           SUVA          ".
02   FILLER PIC X(29) VALUE "E15FINLAND        HELSINKI      ".
02   FILLER PIC X(29) VALUE "E06FRANCE         PARIS         ".
02   FILLER PIC X(29) VALUE "N22FRENCH GUIANACAYENNE        ".
```

```
02  FILLER PIC X(29) VALUE "F27GABON          LIBREVILLE   ".
02  FILLER PIC X(29) VALUE "F04GAMBIA         BANJUL       ".
02  FILLER PIC X(29) VALUE "F10GHANA          ACCRA        ".
02  FILLER PIC X(29) VALUE "E19GREECE         ATHENS       ".
02  FILLER PIC X(29) VALUE "N05GUATEMALA      GUATEMALA CTY".
02  FILLER PIC X(29) VALUE "F05GUINEA-BISSAU  BISSAU       ".
02  FILLER PIC X(29) VALUE "N20GUYANA         GEORGETOWN   ".
02  FILLER PIC X(29) VALUE "N12HAITI          PORTAUPRINCE ".
02  FILLER PIC X(29) VALUE "N07HONDURAS       TEGUCIGALPA  ".
02  FILLER PIC X(29) VALUE "A20HONG KONG      HONG KONG    ".
02  FILLER PIC X(29) VALUE "E27HUNGARY        BUDAPEST     ".
02  FILLER PIC X(29) VALUE "E16ICELAND        REYKJAVIK    ".
02  FILLER PIC X(29) VALUE "A14INDIA          NEW DELHI    ".
02  FILLER PIC X(29) VALUE "A31INDONESIA      DJARKARTA    ".
02  FILLER PIC X(29) VALUE "A08IRAN           TEHRAN       ".
02  FILLER PIC X(29) VALUE "A07IRAQ           BAGHDAD      ".
02  FILLER PIC X(29) VALUE "A03ISRAEL         JERUSALEM    ".
02  FILLER PIC X(29) VALUE "E11ITALY          ROME         ".
02  FILLER PIC X(29) VALUE "F08IVORY COAST    ABIDJAN      ".
02  FILLER PIC X(29) VALUE "N11JAMAICA        KINGSTON     ".
02  FILLER PIC X(29) VALUE "A19JAPAN          TOKYO        ".
02  FILLER PIC X(29) VALUE "A05JORDAN         AMMAN        ".
02  FILLER PIC X(29) VALUE "A27KAMPUCHEA      PHNOM-PENH   ".
02  FILLER PIC X(29) VALUE "F23KENYA          NAIROBI      ".
02  FILLER PIC X(29) VALUE "A04LEBONON        BEIRUT       ".
02  FILLER PIC X(29) VALUE "F07LIBERIA        MONROVIA     ".
02  FILLER PIC X(29) VALUE "F17LIBYA          BANGHAZI     ".
02  FILLER PIC X(29) VALUE "E09LUXEMBOURG     LUXEMBOURG   ".
02  FILLER PIC X(29) VALUE "A30MALAYSIA       KUALA LUMPUR ".
02  FILLER PIC X(29) VALUE "F09MALI           BAMAKO       ".
02  FILLER PIC X(29) VALUE "E20MALTA          VALLETTA     ".
02  FILLER PIC X(29) VALUE "F02MAURITANIA     NOUAKCHOTT   ".
02  FILLER PIC X(29) VALUE "N03MEXICO         MEXICO CITY  ".
02  FILLER PIC X(29) VALUE "F01MOROCCO        RABAT        ".
02  FILLER PIC X(29) VALUE "F32MOZAMBIQUE     MAPUTO       ".
02  FILLER PIC X(29) VALUE "F34NAMIBIA        WINDHOEK     ".
02  FILLER PIC X(29) VALUE "A16NEPAL          KATMANDU     ".
02  FILLER PIC X(29) VALUE "E08NETHERLANDS    THE HAGUE    ".
02  FILLER PIC X(29) VALUE "S02NEW ZEALAND    WELLINGTON   ".
02  FILLER PIC X(29) VALUE "N08NICARAGUA      MANAGUA      ".
02  FILLER PIC X(29) VALUE "F14NIGER          NIAMEY       ".
02  FILLER PIC X(29) VALUE "F13NIGERIA        LAGOS        ".
02  FILLER PIC X(29) VALUE "E13NORWAY         OSLO         ".
02  FILLER PIC X(29) VALUE "A21NORTH KOREA    PYONG-YANG   ".
02  FILLER PIC X(29) VALUE "E04N. IRELAND     BELFAST      ".
02  FILLER PIC X(29) VALUE "A12OMAN           MUSCAT       ".
02  FILLER PIC X(29) VALUE "A15PAKISTAN       ISLAMABAD    ".
02  FILLER PIC X(29) VALUE "N10PANAMA         PANAMA CITY  ".
02  FILLER PIC X(29) VALUE "S03PAPUA & N.G.   PORT MORESBY ".
02  FILLER PIC X(29) VALUE "N18PERU           LIMA         ".
02  FILLER PIC X(29) VALUE "A24PHILIPPINES    MANILA       ".
02  FILLER PIC X(29) VALUE "E25POLAND.        WARSAW       ".
02  FILLER PIC X(29) VALUE "E18PORTUGAL       LISBON       ".
02  FILLER PIC X(29) VALUE "N14PUERTO RICO    SAN JUAN     ".
02  FILLER PIC X(29) VALUE "E28ROMANIA        BUCHAREST    ".
02  FILLER PIC X(29) VALUE "A09SAUDI ARABIA   RIYADH       ".
02  FILLER PIC X(29) VALUE "E02SCOTLAND       EDINBURGH    ".
02  FILLER PIC X(29) VALUE "F03SENEGAL        DAKAR        ".
02  FILLER PIC X(29) VALUE "F06SIERRA LEONE   FREETOWN     ".
02  FILLER PIC X(29) VALUE "A32SINGAPORE      SINGAPORE    ".
02  FILLER PIC X(29) VALUE "F22SOMALI         MOGADISHU    ".
```

```
02   FILLER PIC X(29) VALUE "F33SOUTH AFRICA PRETORIA      ".
02   FILLER PIC X(29) VALUE "A22SOUTH KOREA  SEOUL         ".
02   FILLER PIC X(29) VALUE "E17SPAIN        MADRID        ".
02   FILLER PIC X(29) VALUE "F19SUDAN        KHARTOUM      ".
02   FILLER PIC X(29) VALUE "N21SURINAM      PARAMARIBO    ".
02   FILLER PIC X(29) VALUE "E14SWEDEN       STOCKHOLM     ".
02   FILLER PIC X(29) VALUE "E22SWITZERLAND  BERN          ".
02   FILLER PIC X(29) VALUE "A06SYRIA        DAMASCUS      ".
02   FILLER PIC X(29) VALUE "S05TAHITI       PAPEETEE      ".
02   FILLER PIC X(29) VALUE "A23TAIWAN       TAIPEI        ".
02   FILLER PIC X(29) VALUE "F31TANZANIA     DAR ES SALAAM".
02   FILLER PIC X(29) VALUE "A26THAILAND     BANGKOK       ".
02   FILLER PIC X(29) VALUE "A33TIMOR        DILI          ".
02   FILLER PIC X(29) VALUE "F11TOGO         LOME          ".
02   FILLER PIC X(29) VALUE "A01TURKEY       ANKARA        ".
02   FILLER PIC X(29) VALUE "F24UGANDA       KAMPALA       ".
02   FILLER PIC X(29) VALUE "N26URUGUAY      MONTEVIDEO    ".
02   FILLER PIC X(29) VALUE "N01U.S.A.       WASHINGTON DC".
02   FILLER PIC X(29) VALUE "E23U.S.S.R.     MOSCOW        ".
02   FILLER PIC X(29) VALUE "N15VENEZUELA    CARACOS       ".
02   FILLER PIC X(29) VALUE "A28VIETNAM      HANOI         ".
02   FILLER PIC X(29) VALUE "E03WALES        CARDIFF       ".
02   FILLER PIC X(29) VALUE "E10WEST GERMANY BONN          ".
02   FILLER PIC X(29) VALUE "A10YEMEN        SAH'A         ".
02   FILLER PIC X(29) VALUE "E29YUGOSLAVIA   BELGRADE      ".
02   FILLER PIC X(29) VALUE "F25ZAIRE        KINSHASA      ".
02   FILLER PIC X(29) VALUE "F30ZAMBIA       LUSAKA        ".
02   FILLER PIC X(29) VALUE "F35ZIMBABWE     HARARE        ".
```

Fig. 11.4

required to find a particular country and capital city from a given country code, the search would entail examining each entry in the table in turn. If the matching country code is found the search can cease; if not, the search continues until successful or until the possibilities have been exhausted. For example

```
01   SUBS           PIC 99.
01   WANTED-CODE    PIC XXX.
        .
        .
     MOVE 0 TO SUBS.
SEARCH-LOOP.
     ADD 1 TO SUBS.
     IF SUBS > 129 GO TO MISMATCH. (entry not found)
     IF  WANTED-CODE  NOT  =  COUNTRY-CODE
     (SUBS) GO TO SEARCH-LOOP.
        .
        :  (entry found)
        .
     MOVE COUNTRY-NAME (SUBS) . . .
        .
```

Searching the table for a particular entry can be speeded up if the table is organised so that it is stored in key sequence. Figure 11.5

150

```cobol
01  COUNTRY-LIST.
    02  FILLER PIC X(29) VALUE "A01TURKEY        ANKARA        ".
    02  FILLER PIC X(29) VALUE "A02CYPRUS        NICOSIA       ".
    02  FILLER PIC X(29) VALUE "A03ISRAEL        JERUSALEM     ".
    02  FILLER PIC X(29) VALUE "A04LEBONON       BEIRUT        ".
    02  FILLER PIC X(29) VALUE "A05JORDAN        AMMAN         ".
    02  FILLER PIC X(29) VALUE "A06SYRIA         DAMASCUS      ".
    02  FILLER PIC X(29) VALUE "A07IRAQ          BAGHDAD       ".
    02  FILLER PIC X(29) VALUE "A08IRAN          TEHRAN        ".
    02  FILLER PIC X(29) VALUE "A09SAUDI ARABIA RIYADH         ".
    02  FILLER PIC X(29) VALUE "A10YEMEN         SAH'A         ".
    02  FILLER PIC X(29) VALUE "A12OMAN          MUSCAT        ".
    02  FILLER PIC X(29) VALUE "A13AFGHANISTAN   KABUL         ".
    02  FILLER PIC X(29) VALUE "A14INDIA         NEW DELHI     ".
    02  FILLER PIC X(29) VALUE "A15PAKISTAN      ISLAMABAD     ".
    02  FILLER PIC X(29) VALUE "A16NEPAL         KATMANDU      ".
    02  FILLER PIC X(29) VALUE "A17BANGLADESH    DACCA         ".
    02  FILLER PIC X(29) VALUE "A18CHINA         PEKING        ".
    02  FILLER PIC X(29) VALUE "A19JAPAN         TOKYO         ".
    02  FILLER PIC X(29) VALUE "A20HONG KONG     HONG KONG     ".
    02  FILLER PIC X(29) VALUE "A21NORTH KOREA   PYONG-YANG    ".
    02  FILLER PIC X(29) VALUE "A22SOUTH KOREA   SEOUL         ".
    02  FILLER PIC X(29) VALUE "A23TAIWAN        TAIPEI        ".
    02  FILLER PIC X(29) VALUE "A24PHILIPPINES   MANILA        ".
    02  FILLER PIC X(29) VALUE "A25BURMA         RANGOON       ".
    02  FILLER PIC X(29) VALUE "A26THAILAND      BANGKOK       ".
    02  FILLER PIC X(29) VALUE "A27KAMPUCHEA     PHNOM-PENH    ".
    02  FILLER PIC X(29) VALUE "A28VIETNAM       HANOI         ".
    02  FILLER PIC X(29) VALUE "A29BHUTAN        THIMPHU       ".
    02  FILLER PIC X(29) VALUE "A30MALAYSIA      KUALA LUMPUR  ".
    02  FILLER PIC X(29) VALUE "A31INDONESIA     DJARKARTA     ".
    02  FILLER PIC X(29) VALUE "A32SINGAPORE     SINGAPORE     ".
    02  FILLER PIC X(29) VALUE "A33TIMOR         DILI          ".
    02  FILLER PIC X(29) VALUE "E01ENGLAND       LONDON        ".
    02  FILLER PIC X(29) VALUE "E02SCOTLAND      EDINBURGH     ".
    02  FILLER PIC X(29) VALUE "E03WALES         CARDIFF       ".
    02  FILLER PIC X(29) VALUE "E04N. IRELAND    BELFAST       ".
    02  FILLER PIC X(29) VALUE "E05EIRE          DUBLIN        ".
    02  FILLER PIC X(29) VALUE "E06FRANCE        PARIS         ".
    02  FILLER PIC X(29) VALUE "E07BELGIUM       BRUSSELLS     ".
    02  FILLER PIC X(29) VALUE "E08NETHERLANDS   THE HAGUE     ".
    02  FILLER PIC X(29) VALUE "E09LUXEMBOURG    LUXEMBOURG    ".
    02  FILLER PIC X(29) VALUE "E10WEST GERMANY BONN           ".
    02  FILLER PIC X(29) VALUE "E11ITALY         ROME          ".
    02  FILLER PIC X(29) VALUE "E12DENMARK       COPENHAGEN    ".
    02  FILLER PIC X(29) VALUE "E13NORWAY        OSLO          ".
    02  FILLER PIC X(29) VALUE "E14SWEDEN        STOCKHOLM     ".
    02  FILLER PIC X(29) VALUE "E15FINLAND       HELSINKI      ".
    02  FILLER PIC X(29) VALUE "E16ICELAND       REYKJAVIK     ".
    02  FILLER PIC X(29) VALUE "E17SPAIN         MADRID        ".
    02  FILLER PIC X(29) VALUE "E18PORTUGAL      LISBON        ".
    02  FILLER PIC X(29) VALUE "E19GREECE        ATHENS        ".
    02  FILLER PIC X(29) VALUE "E20MALTA         VALLETTA      ".
    02  FILLER PIC X(29) VALUE "E21AUSTRIA       VIENNA        ".
    02  FILLER PIC X(29) VALUE "E22SWITZERLAND   BERN          ".
    02  FILLER PIC X(29) VALUE "E23U.S.S.R.      MOSCOW        ".
    02  FILLER PIC X(29) VALUE "E24EAST GERMANY BERLIN         ".
    02  FILLER PIC X(29) VALUE "E25POLAND        WARSAW        ".
    02  FILLER PIC X(29) VALUE "E26CZECHOSLOVAK.PRAGUE         ".
    02  FILLER PIC X(29) VALUE "E27HUNGARY       BUDAPEST      ".
    02  FILLER PIC X(29) VALUE "E28ROMANIA       BUCHAREST     ".
```

```cobol
       02  FILLER PIC X(29) VALUE "E29YUGOSLAVIA   BELGRADE      ".
       02  FILLER PIC X(29) VALUE "E30ALBANIA      TIRANA        ".
       02  FILLER PIC X(29) VALUE "F01MOROCCO      RABAT         ".
       02  FILLER PIC X(29) VALUE "F02MAURITANIA   NOUAKCHOTT    ".
       02  FILLER PIC X(29) VALUE "F03SENEGAL      DAKAR         ".
       02  FILLER PIC X(29) VALUE "F04GAMBIA       BANJUL        ".
       02  FILLER PIC X(29) VALUE "F05GUINEA-BISSAUBISSAU        ".
       02  FILLER PIC X(29) VALUE "F06SIERRA LEONE FREETOWN      ".
       02  FILLER PIC X(29) VALUE "F07LIBERIA      MONROVIA      ".
       02  FILLER PIC X(29) VALUE "F08IVORY COAST  ABIDJAN       ".
       02  FILLER PIC X(29) VALUE "F09MALI         BAMAKO        ".
       02  FILLER PIC X(29) VALUE "F10GHANA        ACCRA         ".
       02  FILLER PIC X(29) VALUE "F11TOGO         LOME          ".
       02  FILLER PIC X(29) VALUE "F12BENIN        PORTO NOVO    ".
       02  FILLER PIC X(29) VALUE "F13NIGERIA      LAGOS         ".
       02  FILLER PIC X(29) VALUE "F14NIGER        NIAMEY        ".
       02  FILLER PIC X(29) VALUE "F15CHAD         N'DJAMENA     ".
       02  FILLER PIC X(29) VALUE "F16ALGERIA      ALGIERS       ".
       02  FILLER PIC X(29) VALUE "F17LIBYA        BANGHAZI      ".
       02  FILLER PIC X(29) VALUE "F18EGYPT        CAIRO         ".
       02  FILLER PIC X(29) VALUE "F19SUDAN        KHARTOUM      ".
       02  FILLER PIC X(29) VALUE "F20CENT AFR REP.BANGUI        ".
       02  FILLER PIC X(29) VALUE "F21ETHIOPIA     ADDIS ABABA   ".
       02  FILLER PIC X(29) VALUE "F22SOMALI       MOGADISHU     ".
       02  FILLER PIC X(29) VALUE "F23KENYA        NAIROBI       ".
       02  FILLER PIC X(29) VALUE "F24UGANDA       KAMPALA       ".
       02  FILLER PIC X(29) VALUE "F25ZAIRE        KINSHASA      ".
       02  FILLER PIC X(29) VALUE "F26CONGO        BRAZZAVILLE   ".
       02  FILLER PIC X(29) VALUE "F27GABON        LIBREVILLE    ".
       02  FILLER PIC X(29) VALUE "F28CAMEROON     YAOUNDE       ".
       02  FILLER PIC X(29) VALUE "F29ANGOLA       LUANDA        ".
       02  FILLER PIC X(29) VALUE "F30ZAMBIA       LUSAKA        ".
       02  FILLER PIC X(29) VALUE "F31TANZANIA     DAR ES SALAAM".
       02  FILLER PIC X(29) VALUE "F32MOZAMBIQUE   MAPUTO        ".
       02  FILLER PIC X(29) VALUE "F33SOUTH AFRICA PRETORIA      ".
       02  FILLER PIC X(29) VALUE "F34NAMIBIA      WINDHOEK      ".
       02  FILLER PIC X(29) VALUE "F35ZIMBABWE     HARARE        ".
       02  FILLER PIC X(29) VALUE "N01U.S.A.       WASHINGTON DC".
       02  FILLER PIC X(29) VALUE "N02CANADA       OTTAWA        ".
       02  FILLER PIC X(29) VALUE "N03MEXICO       MEXICO CITY   ".
       02  FILLER PIC X(29) VALUE "N04BELIZE       BELMOPAN      ".
       02  FILLER PIC X(29) VALUE "N05GUATEMALA    GUATEMALA CTY".
       02  FILLER PIC X(29) VALUE "N06EL SALVADOR  SAN SALVADOR  ".
       02  FILLER PIC X(29) VALUE "N07HONDURAS     TEGUCIGALPA   ".
       02  FILLER PIC X(29) VALUE "N08NICARAGUA    MANAGUA       ".
       02  FILLER PIC X(29) VALUE "N09COSTA RICA   SAN JOSE      ".
       02  FILLER PIC X(29) VALUE "N10PANAMA       PANAMA CITY   ".
       02  FILLER PIC X(29) VALUE "N11JAMAICA      KINGSTON      ".
       02  FILLER PIC X(29) VALUE "N12HAITI        PORTAUPRINCE  ".
       02  FILLER PIC X(29) VALUE "N13DOMINICAN REPDOMINICA      ".
       02  FILLER PIC X(29) VALUE "N14PUERTO RICO  SAN JUAN      ".
       02  FILLER PIC X(29) VALUE "N15VENEZUELA    CARACOS       ".
       02  FILLER PIC X(29) VALUE "N16COLUMBIA     BOGOTA        ".
       02  FILLER PIC X(29) VALUE "N17EQUADOR      QUITO         ".
       02  FILLER PIC X(29) VALUE "N18PERU         LIMA          ".
       02  FILLER PIC X(29) VALUE "N19BRAZIL       BRASILIA      ".
       02  FILLER PIC X(29) VALUE "N20GUYANA       GEORGETOWN    ".
       02  FILLER PIC X(29) VALUE "N21SURINAM      PARAMARIBO    ".
       02  FILLER PIC X(29) VALUE "N22FRENCH GUIANACAYENNE       ".
       02  FILLER PIC X(29) VALUE "N23BOLIVIA      LA PAZ        ".
       02  FILLER PIC X(29) VALUE "N24ARGENTINA    BUENOS AIRES  ".
```

```
02   FILLER PIC X(29) VALUE "N25CHILE          SANTIAGO      ".
02   FILLER PIC X(29) VALUE "N26URUGUAY        MONTEVIDEO    ".
02   FILLER PIC X(29) VALUE "S01AUSTRALIA      CANBERRA      ".
02   FILLER PIC X(29) VALUE "S02NEW ZEALAND    WELLINGTON    ".
02   FILLER PIC X(29) VALUE "S03PAPUA & N.G.   PORT MORESBY  ".
02   FILLER PIC X(29) VALUE "S04FIJI           SUVA          ".
02   FILLER PIC X(29) VALUE "S05TAHITI         PAPEETEE      ".

01   COUNTRY-TABLE  REDEFINES  COUNTRY-LIST.
     02   TABLE     OCCURS 129.
          03   COUNTRY-CODE  PIC XXX.
          03   COUNTRY-NAME  PIC X(13).
          03   CAPITAL-NAME  PIC X(13).
```

Fig. 11.5

shows the same list in country code sequence. Some improvement in searching speed is possible by eliminating unnecessary comparisons when the wanted key is not in the table. For example

```
01  SUBS              PIC 99.
01  WANTED-CODE       PIC XXX.

    MOVE 0 TO SUBS.
SEARCH-LOOP.
    ADD 1 TO SUBS.
    IF SUBS > 129 GO TO MISMATCH. (entry not found)
    IF WANTED-CODE < COUNTRY-CODE (SUBS)
       GO TO MISMATCH    (entry not found)
    IF WANTED-CODE > COUNTRY-CODE (SUBS)
       GO TO SEARCH-LOOP.
    :  (entry found)
    :
```

For large tables such coding is inefficient. If, on average, the required entry is half-way down the table, the search would entail (half the table size) × 3 comparisons. In the example above this would total an average of about 200 compare operations per record looked for. A more efficient method is the binary chop technique. The generalised coding is given in Fig. 11.6.

Figure 11.7 shows the effect of a search for country code E16. The first look is at the mid-point of the table—entry number 65, which is country code F02. As F02 is greater than E16 there is no need to search the bottom half of the table. And so entry number 65 is taken as the new maximum position, or new bottom of table.

The second looks is at the new mid-point—entry number 33, which is country code A33. As A33 is less than the wanted code of E16, the top half of the sub-table can be discarded and entry number 33 is taken as the new minimum position or start point. The third

153

point is at the new mid-point—entry number 49, which contains the required country code of E16.

Each unsuccessful search entails three comparisons, but the over-all figure of eight compare instructions certainly compares very favourably with the 200 or so in the equivalent sequential search.

Of course it may not always be possible to find the required entry in so few iterations every time, but in a table of 100 entries it would be unusual to require more than seven or so searches. Hence for large tables even under the worst conditions the binary chop method is worth adopting. But it is vital to ensure that the table is held in key sequence.

It is also worth emphasising that the greater the number of entries

```
WORKING-STORAGE SECTION.
            .
            .
01   TABLE.
            .

01   TABLE-REDEF   REDEFINES   TABLE.
            02   ...   OCCURS n TIMES.
                       03   TABLE-KEY   PIC ...
                       03   ........
            .
            .
01   MIN          PIC 999.
01   MAX          PIC 999.
01   POINTER      PIC 999.
01   FOUND-SWITCH  PIC 9.
01   TABLE-SIZE    PIC 999.
            .
            .
            .
PROCEDURE DIVISION.
            .
            .
            .
BIN-CHOP-ROUTINE.
         MOVE 0 TO FOUND-SWITCH.
         MOVE 0 TO MIN.
         ADD TABLE-SIZE 1 GIVING MAX.
BIN-CHOP-PARA-2.
         ADD MIN MAX GIVING POINTER.
         DIVIDE 2 INTO POINTER ROUNDED.
         IF POINTER = MAX GO TO BIN-CHOP-EXIT.
         IF KEY = TABLE-KEY (POINTER) GO TO BIN-CHOP-PARA-3.
         IF KEY < TABLE-KEY (POINTER) MOVE POINTER TO MAX ELSE
               MOVE POINTER TO MIN.
         GO TO BIN-CHOP-PARA-2.
BIN-CHOP-PARA-3.
         MOVE 1 TO FOUND-SWITCH.
BIN-CHOP-EXIT.
         EXIT.
```

Fig. 11.6

154

First search   Second search   Third search

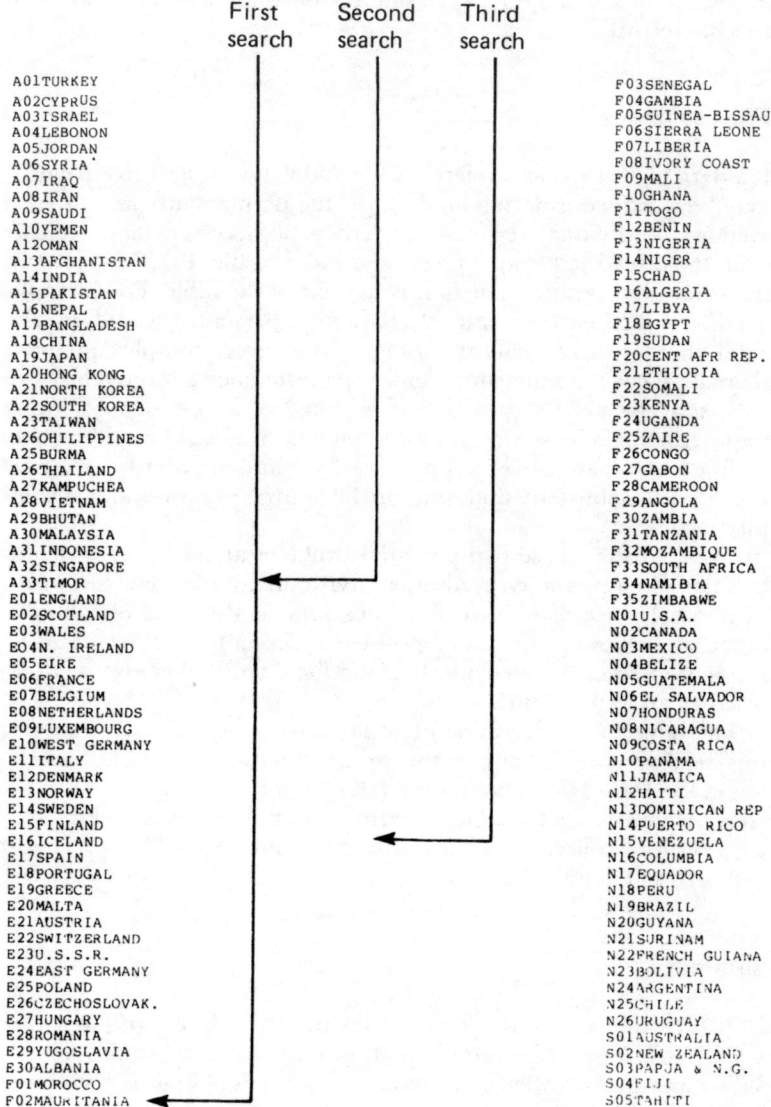

A01TURKEY
A02CYPRUS
A03ISRAEL
A04LEBONON
A05JORDAN
A06SYRIA'
A07IRAQ
A08IRAN
A09SAUDI
A10YEMEN
A12OMAN
A13AFGHANISTAN
A14INDIA
A15PAKISTAN
A16NEPAL
A17BANGLADESH
A18CHINA
A19JAPAN
A20HONG KONG
A21NORTH KOREA
A22SOUTH KOREA
A23TAIWAN
A26OHILIPPINES
A25BURMA
A26THAILAND
A27KAMPUCHEA
A28VIETNAM
A29BHUTAN
A30MALAYSIA
A31INDONESIA
A32SINGAPORE
A33TIMOR
E01ENGLAND
E02SCOTLAND
E03WALES
E04N. IRELAND
E05EIRE
E06FRANCE
E07BELGIUM
E08NETHERLANDS
E09LUXEMBOURG
E10WEST GERMANY
E11ITALY
E12DENMARK
E13NORWAY
E14SWEDEN
E15FINLAND
E16ICELAND
E17SPAIN
E18PORTUGAL
E19GREECE
E20MALTA
E21AUSTRIA
E22SWITZERLAND
E23U.S.S.R.
E24EAST GERMANY
E25POLAND
E26CZECHOSLOVAK.
E27HUNGARY
E28ROMANIA
E29YUGOSLAVIA
E30ALBANIA
F01MOROCCO
F02MAURITANIA

F03SENEGAL
F04GAMBIA
F05GUINEA-BISSAU
F06SIERRA LEONE
F07LIBERIA
F08IVORY COAST
F09MALI
F10GHANA
F11TOGO
F12BENIN
F13NIGERIA
F14NIGER
F15CHAD
F16ALGERIA
F17LIBYA
F18EGYPT
F19SUDAN
F20CENT AFR REP.
F21ETHIOPIA
F22SOMALI
F23KENYA
F24UGANDA
F25ZAIRE
F26CONGO
F27GABON
F28CAMEROON
F29ANGOLA
F30ZAMBIA
F31TANZANIA
F32MOZAMBIQUE
F33SOUTH AFRICA
F34NAMIBIA
F35ZIMBABWE
N01U.S.A.
N02CANADA
N03MEXICO
N04BELIZE
N05GUATEMALA
N06EL SALVADOR
N07HONDURAS
N08NICARAGUA
N09COSTA RICA
N10PANAMA
N11JAMAICA
N12HAITI
N13DOMINICAN REP
N14PUERTO RICO
N15VENEZUELA
N16COLUMBIA
N17EQUADOR
N18PERU
N19BRAZIL
N20GUYANA
N21SURINAM
N22FRENCH GUIANA
N23BOLIVIA
N24ARGENTINA
N25CHILE
N26URUGUAY
S01AUSTRALIA
S02NEW ZEALAND
S03PAPJA & N.G.
S04FIJI
S05TAHITI

Fig. 11.7

155

in the table, the greater the advantage of using a binary search for specific records.

Files as tables

If a data file is used as a reference file and is not subject to change, it may be worth considering holding the file permanently as a table in memory. Individual records could then be accessed more quickly from the table than from a relative or indexed file. But there are two important limitations. The first is the size of the table. For example, a table of 120 entries with 30 characters per entry would require 3600 characters of memory storage. In a large, complex program there may not be sufficient memory space for such a large table, and so it may be necessary to sacrifice speed of access to meet other requirements. The second limitation is that the table would have to be free from change over a long period of time in order to eliminate the need for constant updating of the source program and recompilation.

Provided that these two potential problem areas do not pose difficulties, then in a microcomputer environment it is well worth considering the use of built-in reference files in the form of tables in order to overcome the major problems of relatively slow access at random to records, particularly if the file would otherwise be organised as an indexed file.

The table may have to be incorporated in several programs. But this need not present any major problem because the table, as written in the Data Division, and the table handling routine in the Procedure Division can both be pre-written and placed into a library for copying into source programs at compilation time. This process is explored in Chapter 12.

Summary

COBOL offers excellent table creation facilities through the OCCURS clause, and two methods of table handling, indexing and subscripting. The choice of method of table handling is left to the programmer, though most systems suggest that indexing is to be preferred as it requires less calculation of address positions at run time.

The use of the PERFORM statement to perform out-of-sequence routines, particularly in the formats which control the conditions under which the PERFORM is to be executed, can make table handling very easy. And the technique of binary searching can speed up the access to particular records in large tables.

Self-test questions

1 The Working-Storage Section contains the following entries:

```
01   TOTALS.
     02   BY-AREA      OCCURS 6.
          03   BY-REP   OCCURS 20.
               04   QUANTITY PIC 9(6).
               04   VAL          PIC 9(6)V99.
01   GRAND-QTY   PIC 9(10).
01   GRAND-VAL   PIC 9(10)V99.
01   SUB-A   PIC 9.
01   SUB-R   PIC 99.
```

What coding might be used to add the contents of all QUANTITY and GRAND-QTY and all VAL to GRAND-VAL assuming that subscripts are used, and using the following methods:
(a) PERFORM . . . VARYING.
(b) PERFORM n TIMES.
(c) PERFORM UNTIL . . .
(d) The PERFORM statement is not used.

2 Rewrite the Working-Storage and Procedure Division entries given in question 1 above on the basis that indexing is used instead of subscripting.

3 What is a binary chop procedure and how does it work?

12
COBOL source library

One of the more useful facilities in any programming system is the ability to incorporate pre-written standard text into a program. The uses can vary from having a standard file description, which is incorporated in all programs using that file, to having a program written, perhaps by several people, in the form of a series of modules which can then be linked together to form a single program.

This is achieved through the use of a COBOL source library. A source library is quite simply a piece of COBOL source coding such as a file description or Procedure Division routine written and stored on disc as a separate entity. For example, the following entry may be written as a source library file.

```
01   PRODUCT-RECORD.
     02   PRODUCT-NO      PIC X(5).
     02   PRODUCT-DESC    PIC X(20).
     02   PRODUCT-PRICE   PIC 9(4)V99.
     02   PRODUCT-QTY     PIC 9(6).
     02   PRODUCT-DATE.
          03   PRODUCT-YEAR    PIC 99.
          03   PRODUCT-MONTH   PIC 99.
          03   PRODUCT-DAY     PIC 99.
```

This is a conventional record description and has been used elsewhere in this book. It can be written as a CP/M file in the same way as any COBOL source program by means of word processing package or text editor and stored on disc. The source library entry must be given a name, using the rules pertaining to file names, such as PROD.LIB.

When the programmer writes a source program which requires that particular record description, instead of writing

```
01   PRODUCT-RECORD.
          :
     03   PRODUCT-DAY    PIC 99.
```

he can simply write

COPY "PROD.LIB".

instead. The word COPY must start in position 12 or later (Area B of the COBOL coding form), the name of the source library must be bounded by quotation marks, and the entry must end with a period.

The COPY may be used in the Environment Division, to create standardised file select entries for example, and in the Procedure Division for standardised routines, such as the binary chop routine listed in the last chapter.

The text of the source library is copied unchanged and becomes part of the source program at compilation time. However, the text which forms the source library is not itself printed at compilation time unless specifically requested in the compilation command. In the case of CIS COBOL the compilation command might read

A>COBOL UPDT.CBL LIST(:LP:)

To have the COBOL source entries listed would require the COPYLIST parameter to be specified, so that the compilation command would read

A>COBOL UPDT.CBL COPYLIST LIST(:LP:)

Other compilers have similar facilities and commands.

A major advantage of using COBOL source library is seen in the problems associated with changing such entries as record descriptions. If COBOL source library is not used, each program using the changed record descriptions would have to be amended manually. Such amendment carries the risk that the amendment may not be carried out correctly in all programs and that some programs may not be changed.

If COBOL source is used, only the library need be changed and the source programs recompiled. The programs in their newly compiled forms will reflect the changes made in the library. However, the use of COBOL source library still requires that all programs using the amended library entry be recompiled. And there may be Procedure Division changes to be made to individual programs to reflect changes to the record description.

A further advantage of using COBOL source library is that valuable disc storage space is not occupied by repeated source coding.

Looking ahead, particularly as new facilities become available in microcomputer COBOL, it is likely that the COPY facility will be extended to allow text in the source library to be copied across, but incorporating some changes. This might lead to a COPY statement which is written

COPY 'PROD.LIB' REPLACING 'PRODUCT' BY 'PAPER'.

in which case the text in the program would read

```
01  PAPER-RECORD.
    02  PAPER-NO   PIC X(5)
        :
```

and so on.

Summary

A COBOL source library allows standard COBOL text to be written and stored on disc in the same way as standard source programs. Source library can be incorporated in any COBOL source program in place of the text which constitutes the library. This facility enables standard coding to be prepared and eases the burden of program writing and amendment.

13
Program debugging

COBOL provides for the monitoring of procedures as they are executed in order to debug, or trade and eliminate errors from the program. The program can be compiled so that it includes debugging routines and a special register that contains information about the conditions which caused the execution of the debugging routines. We will first consider the actual COBOL coding that needs to be written and then look at how it may be used.

Environment Division coding is used to indicate whether the debugging facilities are to be included when the program is compiled. The coding used to include the debugging facilities is

    ENVIRONMENT DIVISION.
    CONFIGURATION SECTION.
    SOURCE-COMPUTER. MODEL-XYZ WITH
        DEBUGGING MODE.

Specifying DEBUGGING MODE in this manner causes all Procedure Division debugging elements to be compiled as object code. The omission of the clause would cause those Procedure Division elements to be treated as though they were comment lines—printed on the source program listing but not capable of being activated.

The actual activation of the debug facility comes at run time. The manner of invoking the debugging facilities varies from one version of COBOL to another. In the case of CIS COBOL it is invoked by entering (+D) as a parameter in the RUN command immediately before the program name. For example, if the program UPDT.INT is to be run with the debugging facilities the command would take the form

    A>RUN (+D) UPDT.INT

Debug item

There is no specific Data Division coding as such for debugging. However, the debugging facility uses a special register which is treated as though it were declared in the Working-Storage Section of the Data Division as follows:

```
01  DEBUG-ITEM.
    02  DEBUG-LINE    PIC X(6).
    02  FILLER        PIC X VALUE SPACE.
    02  DEBUG-NAME    PIC X(30).
    02  FILLER        PIC X VALUE SPACE.
    02  DEBUG-SUB-1   PIC S9(4) SIGN IS LEADING
        SEPARATE CHARACTER.
    02  FILLER        PIC X VALUE SPACE.
    02  DEBUG-SUB-2   PIC S9(4) SIGN IS LEADING
        SEPARATE CHARACTER.
    02  FILLER             PIC X VALUE SPACE.
    02  DEBUG-SUB-3        PIC  S9(4)  SIGN  IS
    LEADING
        SEPARATE CHARACTER.
    02  FILLER             PIC X VALUE SPACE.
    02  DEBUG-CONTENTS PIC X(n).
```

The program may directly reference these data names in the debugging sections even though they have not been explicitly declared.

Declaratives

Procedure Division coding will start with a special element called DECLARATIVES. The coding takes the form

```
PROCEDURE DIVISION.
DECLARATIVES.
DEBUG-ROUTINE SECTION. USE FOR DEBUGGING
    ON MAIN-PARA-X.
DEBUG-PARA.
        ⋮  debugging routine
        ⋮
END DECLARATIVES.
```

All the debugging procedures must appear together immediately after the DECLARATIVES header and must be self-contained in that they must not reference procedures which are outside the debugging sections. That is, the debugging routine may contain PERFORM and GO TO instructions so long as these instructions pass control to other debugging procedures. For example

```
DECLARATIVES.
```

```
DEBUG-ROUTINE SECTION.    USE FOR DEBUGGING
    ON MAIN-PROG-X.
DEBUG-PARA-A.
    IF DEBUG-LINE NOT = "020610" GO TO
        DEBUG-PARA-B.
    DISPLAY "ITS GONE AGAIN AT 020610".
    GO TO DEBUG-PARA-X.
DEBUG-PARA-B.
    DISPLAY DEBUG-LINE.
DEBUG-PARA-X.
    EXIT.
END DECLARATIVES.
```

Entry into the debugging section is brought about by a routine in the main body of the program, control passing to a paragraph called **MAIN-PROG-X**. But within the debugging section the GO TOs refer to **DEBUG-PARA-B** and **DEBUG-PARA-X** which are paragraphs within the debugging procedures.

Within the **USE** statement reference can be made either to a procedure name in the main body of the Procedure Division or to ALL PROCEDURES. For example

```
DECLARATIVES.
DEBUG-ROUTINE SECTION. USE FOR DEBUGGING ON
    ALL PROCEDURES.

    .
    .
```

If the statement **ALL PROCEDURES** is used, then only that statement can appear for debugging purposes, and the debugging routines will be invoked whenever program control passes to a new procedure name in the Procedure Division.

But there may be multiple **USE** statements referencing different procedure names if the **ALL PROCEDURES** is not specified. This makes the debugging facility more selective. For example

```
DECLARATIVES.
DEBUG-ROUTINE-A SECTION. USE FOR DEBUGGING
    ON MAIN-PROGRAM-PARA-1.
DEBUG-PARA-A.
        .
        .

DEBUG-B-SECTION. USE FOR DEBUGGING ON
    MAIN-PROGRAM-PRINT-PARA.
DEBUG-PARA-B.
        .
        .

END DECLARATIVES.
```

If a specific main program procedure is named in the USE statement, such as MAIN-PROGRAM-PARA-1 and MAIN-PROGRAM-PRINT-PARA in the example above, the debugging section is entered and executed immediately that procedure is entered but before the execution of the first statement in that procedure. For example

DECLARATIVES.
DEBUG-ROUTINE SECTION. USE FOR DEBUGGING
ON CALC-PAY.
DEBUG-PARA.
    :

END DECLARATIVES.
BEGIN.
    OPEN . . .
READ-EMPLOYER-RECORD.
    READ . . .
        :

CALC-PAY.
    IF PAY-TYPE = "W" GO TO WEEKLY-PAID.
        :

In this case, as soon as the run-time monitor identifies that the paragraph CALC-PAY has been entered it passes control to the debug routine for execution before going on to the

IF PAY-TYPE . . .

instruction.

Furthermore, the control will pass to the debug routines every time that paragraph is entered. So if the debug command is

USE FOR DEBUGGING ON MULTIPLY-RATE

and the main program contains the instruction

PERFORM MULTIPLY-RATE 16 TIMES.

then control will pass to the debugging section each of the 16 times.

The first effect of activating the debug routines is that the special register DEBUG-ITEM, mentioned earlier in the chapter, is updated immediately before control passes to the debugging section. DEBUG-ITEM is set to spaces, and its constituent fields are updated according to the following rules:

1. DEBUG-LINE is set to the six-digit source program line number

that caused the debugging section to be invoked, such as the GO TO which sent control to the named procedure.

2. DEBUG-NAME is set to the first 30 characters of the procedure name which caused the debugging section to be invoked. In the case of

USE FOR DEBUGGING ON CALC-PAY.

DEBUG-NAME will contain the characters CALC-PAY.
   Where

USE FOR DEBUGGING ON ALL PROCEDURES.

is specified, the debugging routine will be invoked by all procedure names outside the debugging section itself, and DEBUG-NAME will contain the name of the paragraph just entered.

3. DEBUG-CONTENTS is used as follows:

(a) If the USE statement specifies ON ALL PROCEDURES, then when the program enters the first main program paragraph for the first time DEBUG-CONTENTS is set to 'START PROGRAM'.

(b) If the program falls through into the named procedure in a USE . . . ON PARA-X, it is set to 'FALL THROUGH'.

(c) If USE . . . ON PARA-X is specified in the debugging section and the paragraph PARA-X is referred to in an ALTER statement, such as

ALTER PARA-X TO PROCEED TO PAYE-ROUTINE.

then DEBUG-line will contain the source program line number of the ALTER statement, DEBUG-NAME the name of the procedure which caused the debug section to be invoked, and DEBUG-CONTENTS the name of the paragraph last named in the ALTER (PAYE-ROUTINE in this example).

(d) If control passes to the debug section through the execution of a PERFORM, then DEBUG-CONTENTS will be set to 'PERFORM LOOP'.

(e) IF USE . . . ON PROCEDURE-NAME-A is specified, and PROCEDURE-NAME-A is a procedure name specified in a USE statement elsewhere in DECLARATIVES (it might for example be associated with file handling procedures) then DEBUG-CONTENTS will be set to 'USE PROCEDURE'.

4. The rest of DEBUG-ITEM is normally set to spaces.

Debugging lines

COBOL permits debugging to take place without the need to set up a DECLARATIVES entry. Such debugging takes place through debugging lines. A debugging line is an optional line that can produce object coding at the user's discretion. Debugging lines follow these rules:

(a) A debugging line is recognised as being such by having a "D" in column 7 (the indicator area of the source line).
(b) The debugging line is activated as a debugging line if the program is compiled with the statement

> SOURCE-COMPUTER. MODEL-XYZ WITH
> DEBUGGING MODE.

The absence of this coding causes the debugging line to be treated as though it were a comment line, that is its procedures will not be actioned.
(c) The debugging lines may appear anywhere in the source program after the OBJECT-COMPUTER paragraph and must be syntactically correct even if the lines are treated as though they were comment lines.
(d) Any number of successive debugging lines is permitted, each having "D" in column 7.
(e) If the debugging lines are not to be activated, the program must be compiled without the WITH DEBUGGING MODE in the SOURCE-COMPUTER paragraph.

This facility is useful when testing programs in that it may not be desired to go through possibly lengthy and complex USE procedures. For example, the programmer may wish to do no more than have the program display a message and/or a value on the VDU screen whenever a certain instruction is executed. It can be simpler to incorporate DISPLAY instructions, for example, at predetermined debug points than to work on a system of debugging only on entry into specific procedures.

CIS COBOL interactive debugging

In addition to the ANSI standard debugging facilities, CIS COBOL provides its own run-time interactive debugging facilities which can be specified at run time without any special source program coding.

When a compiled program is listed, each Procedure Division statement has its memory storage address relative to the start of the

Procedure Division printed at the right-hand side (see Fig. 13.1). At run time the operator enters the program name and the command +D to activate the program and the CIS COBOL interactive module; for example

A>RUN +D UPDT.INT

The system will return a question mark (?) as a prompt message, and the user can then specify the debugging action. When the debugging action has been completed the ? prompt reappears. There are about a dozen debug commands available under the system. The more commonly used ones would probably be:

(a) G and an address, for example G 0102, which causes the system to execute the program from its current position in its normal manner until the specified 'breakpoint' is reached, that is until the instruction at the specified address is encountered. At this point the program will halt and a new ? prompt issued. It is important to note that action is taken, i.e. the program halts, only when the specified breakpoint address is reached. If the address is not met then the debug command will not be activated.

```
* CIS COBOL V4.2              LOAD.CBL                    PAGE: 0001
**
010000 IDENTIFICATION DIVISION.                                0118
010100 PROGRAM-ID.   LOAD.                                     0118
010200 ENVIRONMENT DIVISION.                                   0118
010300 CONFIGURATION SECTION.                                  0118
010400 SOURCE-COMPUTER.    MODEL-XYZ.                           0118
010500 OBJECT-COMPUTER.    MODEL-XYZ.                           0118
010600 INPUT-OUTPUT SECTION.                                   0118
010700 FILE-CONTROL.                                           0118
010800     SELECT PRODUCT-FILE ASSIGN TO "PRODUCT.DAT"         0176
010900         ORGANIZATION INDEXED  ACCESS SEQUENTIAL         0176
011000         RECORD KEY   PRODUCT-KEY.                       0176
011100     SELECT IN-FILE ASSIGN TO "TEMP.DAT"                 01A5
011200         ORGANIZATION LINE SEQUENTIAL.                   01A5
020000 DATA DIVISION.                                          01D4
020100 FILE SECTION.                                           01D4
020200 FD   PRODUCT-FILE.                                      01D4
020300 01   PRODUCT-REC.                                       01D4
020400     02   PRODUCT-KEY   PIC X(5).                        01D4
020500     02   FILLER        PIC X(36).                       01D9
020600 FD   IN-FILE.                                           01FF
020700 01   IN-REC    PIC X(41).                               01FF
030000 PROCEDURE DIVISION.                                     0000
030100 BEGIN.                                                  0023
030200     OPEN INPUT IN-FILE                                  0024
030300          OUTPUT PRODUCT-FILE.                           0024
030400 READ-PRODUCT.                                           002C
030500     READ IN-FILE AT END GO TO FINISH.                  002D
030600     MOVE IN-REC TO PRODUCT-REC.                         0039
030700     WRITE PRODUCT-REC.                                  0042
030800     GO TO READ-PRODUCT.                                 0045
030900 FINISH.                                                 0048
031000     CLOSE PRODUCT-FILE IN-FILE.                         0049
031100     STOP RUN.                                           0051
                                                               0052
** CIS COBOL V4.2 COMPILER COPYRIGHT (C) 1979 MICRO FOCUS LTD URN AA/0487/BL
**
**ERRORS=00000 DATA=00554 CODE=00117 DICT=00234:17901        END OF LIST
```

Fig. 13.1

(b) T and an address, for example T 0143. This will cause the program to be executed until the breakpoint address is reached at which time the program will halt and another ? prompt issued. However, it will also display on the VDU the address of the first statement in each new paragraph as it is entered. It thus provides a trace at paragraph name level. The memory address of the procedure is displayed at the left-hand side of the VDU screen.

(c) The X command causes the next COBOL statement to be executed. The result of this is that the instruction is executed, the address of the following instruction (the one about to be executed) is displayed on the VDU screen, followed by a ? prompt on the next line. This command enables an instruction-by-instruction trace to be carried out, and can also help in informing the user of the effects of an instruction on data entries. This is achieved with the aid of the next command.

(d) The D and address command. The Data Division entries on the source program listing also have memory storage addresses printed alongside the source coding. The D command tells the run time system to display on the VDU screen 16 bytes starting at the specified data entry address as given in the source listing. Each of the 16 bytes is displayed both in its hexadecimal form and in its ASCII character equivalent. Thus a G command can be used to halt the program at a specific breakpoint, a D command can then be used to display the conents of a data item, X commands can then be used to cause further COBOL statements to be executed, and then a further D command issued to see what the new contents of the data item are.

(e) The S command enables the user to load the address of a data item into a work register. For example

S 02AA

will put the address 02AA into a working register and causes another ? prompt to be issued. This may be followed by a command to enter new contents (in hexadecimal form). For example

?S 02AA
?.46.52.45.44
?

This will cause the hexadecimal value 46 to be put into 02AA, 52 to be put in 02AB, 45 into 02AC, and 44 into 02AD. The '.' causes the contents to be amended and the address in the working register incremented by one.

168

Summary

The debugging aids provided by COBOL help with the debugging of programs. These aids come at a number of levels and are designed to enable the user to trace the progress of the program through its various procedures. In addition, at the various breakpoints, instructions can be given to enable the contents of data areas to be displayed, or even modified.

COBOL provides for the specification of debugging at the time the program is compiled, although the command that debugging is to be carried out is given at run time.

CIS COBOL takes the debugging process a stage further in that it permits the program to be the subject of debugging routines even though no debugging requirement was specified at compilation time. The interactive debugging commands are short and simple to use, though for best effect require that the listing of the program being executed is available at the time the program is running in interactive debug mode.

Self-test questions

1 What are debugging lines? How are they identified in the source program? How are they activated?

2 What is the function of a DEBUG-ITEM?

3 What is the function of DECLARATIVES?

4 The debugging procesures in a program contain the statement.

> DEBUGGING-PROC SECTION. USE FOR DEBUGGING ON ALL PROCEDURES.

When is the debugging procedure entered?

5 What is wrong with the following coding?

DEBUG-ROUTINE 1 SECTION. USE FOR DEBUGGING ON
    ALL PROCEDURES.
DEBUG-PARA.
    DISPLAY DEBUG-ITEM.
DEBUG-ROUTINE-2 SECTION. USE FOR DEBUGGING
    ON MAIN-PROC-A.
DEBUG-PARA-2.
    DISPLAY "ERROR ON PROC" AT 0301.
    DISPLAY DEBUG-LINE AT 0401.

14
Program segmentation

It does happen on occasion that on compilation the object program proves to be too large to be accommodated in the available memory storage area. By using more efficient programming techniques it may be possible to reduce the size of the program. For example it may be possible to incorporate some of the following suggestions.

(a) When processing tables of data using indexing, because on most computers table handling is more efficiently handled by indexing than by subscripting.
(b) If subscripting is used, eliminate the use of the subscripts as far as possible. For example, if the same subscripted data item is referenced several times it is more efficient to move the contents of the subscripted data item to an elementary data field and use that data field instead in this manner:

    MOVE TABLE-ENTRY (SUBS) TO WORK1.
    MOVE WORK1 TO ...
          :
    IF WORK1 ...

The reason for this is that each time a subscripted data item is referenced additional coding is generated to calculate the actual position in the table.
(c) Keep the number of digits in numeric fields as small as possible, and use USAGE COMP or COMP-3 as much as possible for elementary numeric data items.
(d) Use group moves, accepts and displays rather than a series of elementary moves, accepts and displays. This cuts down the number of statements.

If despite all efforts at space saving the object program is still too large, then it will be necessary to segment it. By this we mean that the Procedure Division instructions are grouped into a series of sections, of which only some are permanently resident in memory during the running of the program, the others being called into memory as and when required. It is important to note that the Data Division cannot be segmented.

The programs listed in the earlier chapters of this book have not contained Procedure Division sections except where DECLARATIVES was specified. However, segmented programs must be written in sections, with each section being given a segment number.

The segment numbers serve two purposes:

(a) To indicate which sections are part of the fixed or permanently resident portion of the program and which are independent or transient sections which may be overlaid by other independent sections.

(b) To indicate which sections are to form a common segment. Thus all sections with, say, segment number 60 are treated as a common segment and will be loaded into memory together.

When using segmentation the peculiarities of the particular COBOL compiler must be taken into account. It is common to have the following Environment Division entry.

OBJECT-COMPUTER. MODEL-XYZ SEGMENT-LIMIT
   10.

where the number following SEGMENT-LIMIT (10 in this case) is a priority number of up to 50. All the sections with a segment number lower than the priority number (0–9 in this example) constitute the resident part of the Procedure Division.

However, CIS COBOL does not use the SEGMENT-LIMIT statement. Instead all sections with a segment number of between 0 and 49 constitute the fixed portion of the program; sections with segment number of between 50 and 99 constitute the independent portion.

Writing a segmented Procedure Division is no more difficult than writing a non-segmented program. But the following rules should be followed:

1. The sequence of the Procedure Division is always to have the fixed portion placed at the beginning, and this is followed by the independent portion. For example

PROCEDURE DIVISION.
FIXED-PORTION SECTION 01.
PARA-A.
   :

PARA-B.
   :

IND-PORTION-A SECTION 50.
PARA-X1.
   :

PARA-X2.

    :

IND-PORTION-B SECTION 51.
PARA-X10.

    :

2. If declaratives are used, their segment numbers must be between 0 and 49, that is they must be in the fixed portion of the program. For example

PROCEDURE DIVISION.
DECLARATIVES.
DEBUG-BIT SECTION 01. USE FOR DEBUGGING ON
   MAIN-PROC-06.
DEBUG-PARAGRAPH.

    :

END DECLARATIVES.
MAIN-PROC-01 SECTION 01.
MAIN-PARA.

    :

MAIN-PROC-02 SECTION 01.
MAIN-PARA-2.

    :

MAIN-PROC-06 SECTION 10.
MAIN-PARA-3.

    :

3. If a section is in the fixed portion, the segment number need not be specified. If it is not specified the compiler will allocate it the segment number 0. This means that in practice it is not necessary to specify segment numbers in Declaratives.

4. An independent segment is in its initial state, that is unaffected by the execution of ALTER and PERFORM statements, the first time control is passed to it.

5. An independent segment is also in its initial state when control passes to it implicitly through a fall-through from a preceding section with a different segment number. For example, in the case of

PROCESS-XYZ SECTION 60.
PARA-XYZ.

    :

PROCESS-PAYX SECTION 61.
PARA-PAYX.

    :

if control passes through from PROCESS-XYZ to PROCESS-PAYX then PROCESS-PAYX is set to its initial state when it is

172

brought into memory. It would be wise to read about the initial state and the effects of switch setting in the programming manual for the particular version of COBOL as different compilers treat fixed and independent segments differently.

6. The more frequently used procedures should be put into the fixed portion of the program in order to avoid the time-consuming process of segment loading from disc. On the other hand, rarely used procedures are best written as independent segments to be loaded into memory storage as and when required.

7. A GO TO statement in a section with a segment number of between 50 and 99 must not be referred to in an ALTER statement in a section with a different segment number. Thus

    PROC-X SECTION 60.
    PARA-X.
        .
        ALTER PARA-Y2 TO PROCEED TO PARA-Y5.

    PROC-Y SECTION 70.
    PARA-Y1.
        .

    PARA-Y2.
        GO TO PARA-Y4.
    PARA-Y3.
        .

    PARA-Y4.
        .

    PARA-Y5.
        .

is illegal.

8. A PERFORM statement in a permanent segment can specify only either procedures wholly contained within the permanent portion or procedures wholly contained within a single independent segment. For example

    MAIN-PROC-01 SECTION 10.
    MAIN-01.
        .
        PERFORM MAIN-17 THROUGH MAIN-24.

    MAIN-PROC-02 SECTION 10.
    MAIN-02.
        .

    MAIN-PROC-05 SECTION 10.

    MAIN-15.
        .

    MAIN 17.
        .

MAIN 20.

MAIN-24.

MAIN-PROC-03 SECTION 10.
MAIN-30.

is legal, and so is

MAIN-PROC-01 SECTION 10.
MAIN-01.

    PERFORM IND-PROC-04.

MAIN-PROC-02 SECTION 10.
MAIN-02.

IND-PROC-04 SECTION 50.
IND-04.

IND-PROC-05 SECTION 52.
IND-05.

whereas, using the last example,

    PERFORM IND-PROC-04 THRU IND-PROC-05

is illegal as these procedure names have different segment numbers.
9. A PERFORM statement within an independent segment (50–99)
may reference only procedures in sections with the same segment
number.

Summary

Segmentation is a procedure used to reduce the amount of memory
storage required by an object program. All the data areas and the
Procedure Division sections with segment numbers between 0 and
49 are permanently resident during the running of the program. The
sections with segment numbers of between 50 and 99 constitute
independent segments which are called into memory as and when
required, with all sections having the same segment number being
loaded into memory at the same time.

    There are some restrictions on the passing of control from one seg-
ment to another in PERFORM statements, but these restrictions are
fairly minimal. Perhaps a more important limitation could be the
time it takes to load an independent segment.

15
Inter-program communication

COBOL provides the means whereby control can be passed from one program to another, and enables both programs to use common data. In order to achieve this inter-program communication special entries have to be made in both the Data Division and the Procedure Division.

Data Division Linkage Section

The Data Division has a section called the Linkage Section which is used to describe the data defined in a calling program that is to be made available to the called program. This is data which is used in both the calling and the called programs, or the master and slave programs.

The structure of the Linkage Section is similar to that of the Working-Storage Section except that the VALUE clause of Linkage data items must not be specified in the Linkage Section.

Procedure Division

The master calling program transfers control to the called program by means of the CALL statement; for example

CALL "CALLED.INT" USING LINK1 LINK2 VAL1.

The CALL statement references the name of the program to take control. The calling program also specifies any common data items after the word USING. These data items must have been described in the File Section, Working-Storage Section, or Linkage Section of the calling program at level 01 or 77.

The called program must reference the same data items in its Procedure Division header, though it need not use the same data names.

On the first occasion the CALL statement is executed, the called program is in its initial state as called into memory. Subsequent calls to the called program see it in the same state as it was when it finished its last statement. That is, all the data items and switch settings are as they were when control returned to the master calling program.

A called program may itself call another program, but cannot directly or indirectly call the master calling program. The sequence of control is such that control must return eventually to the master calling program following the same route as the outward path. If Program A calls Program B which then calls Program C, which in turn calls Program D, control returns from Program D to Program C, then to Program B and finally to Program A. Though execution of the entire job can be terminated at any stage through the execution of a STOP RUN instruction.

Execution of a called program begins with the first non-declarative statement in the Procedure Division and continues until either a STOP RUN or an EXIT PROGRAM is encountered.

A STOP RUN causes the entire job to terminate; and EXIT PROGRAM returns control to the calling program—to the statement following the CALL. The EXIT PROGRAM statement must appear in a sentence on its own as the only sentence in the paragraph.

The CANCEL statement is used to release the memory areas occupied by the named program. For example, the master calling program may contain the statement

   CANCEL "CALLED1.INT", "CALLED2.INT".

This cancels all relationships between the master calling program and the named programs. This relates to the setting of data values and switches which are normally retained in their old state after a return of control to the master calling program. Thus if CALLED1.INT is cancelled, it may still be called again by a CALL statement issued by the master calling program. But if it is called again it will start with its initial values and switch settings.

If a CANCEL statement is given which references a called program which has not yet been called, or has been called but has subsequently been cancelled, the instruction is ignored and control passes to the statement following the ignored CANCEL.

Figure 15.1 shows an example of a master calling program and 15.2 an example of a program called by the master calling program. The screen layout of the master calling program is shown in Fig. 15.3.

```
001000 IDENTIFICATION DIVISION.
001010 PROGRAM-ID.    CALLING.
001020 ENVIRONMENT DIVISION.
001030 CONIGURATION SECTION.
001040 SOURCE-COMPUTER.  MODEL-XYZ.
001050 OBJECT-COMPUTER.  MODEL-XYZ.
001060 SPECIAL-NAMES.    CONSOLE IS CRT.
001070 DATA DIVISION.
001080 WORKING-STORAGE SECTION.
001090 01  MAIN-MENU.
001100     02   FILLER    PIC X(25).
001110     02   MENU-00-01 PIC X(15) VALUE "XYZ SPORTS CLUB".
001120     02   FILLER    PIC X(168).
001130     02   MENU-00-02 PIC X(9) VALUE "MAIN MENU".
001140     02   FILLER    PIC X(138).
001150     02   MENU-00-03 PIC X(17) VALUE "1  BOOKING SYSTEM".
001160     02   FILLER    PIC X(63).
001170     02   MENU-00-04 PIC X(14) VALUE "2  MISC. SALES".
001180     02   FILLER    PIC X(66).
001190     02   MENU-00-05 PIC X(12) VALUE "3  PURCHASES".
001200     02   FILLER    PIC X(68).
001210     02   MENU-00-06 PIC X(8) VALUE "4  WAGES".
001220     02   FILLER    PIC X(72).
001230     02   MENU-00-07 PIC X(6) VALUE "5  END".
001240     02   FILLER    PIC X(168).
001250     02   MENU-00-08 PIC X(23) VALUE "] [       DATE ] / / [".
001260 01  ENTER-MAIN-MENU  REDEFINES  MAIN-MENU.
001270     02   FILLER    PIC X(830).
001280     02   OPT       PIC 9.
001290     02   FILLER    PIC X(15).
001300     02   DAY       PIC 99.
001310     02   FILLER    PIC X.
001320     02   MONTH     PIC 99.
001330     02   FILLER    PIC X.
001340     02   YEAR      PIC 99.
001350 01  W-DATE.
001360     02   W-DAY     PIC 99.
001370     02   W-MONTH   PIC 99.
001380     02   W-YEAR    PIC 99.
002000 PROCEDURE DIVISION.
002010 BEGIN.
002020     DISPLAY SPACE.
002030     DISPLAY MAIN-MENU.
002040 ENTER-MENU.
002050     ACCEPT ENTER-MAIN-MENU.
002060     IF OPT = 5 STOP RUN.
002070     IF OPT < 1 GO TO ENTER-MENU.
002080     IF OPT > 4 GO TO ENTER-MENU.
002090     IF DAY < 01 GO TO ENTER-MENU.
002100     IF DAY > 31 GO TO ENTER-MENU.
002110     IF MONTH < 01 GO TO ENTER-MENU.
002120     IF MONTH > 12 GO TO ENTER-MENU.
002130     IF YEAR < 83 GO TO ENTER-MENU.
002140     IF YEAR > 90 GO TO ENTER-MENU.
002150     MOVE DAY TO W-DAY.
002160     MOVE MONTH TO W-MONTH.
002170     MOVE YEAR TO W-YEAR.
002180     GO TO BOOKING SALES PURCHASES WAGES DEPENDING ON OPT.
002190 BOOKING.
002200     CALL "BOOKING.INT" USING W-DATE.
002210     GO TO BEGIN.
002220 SALES.
002230     CALL "SALES.INT" USING W-DATE.
002240     GO TO BEGIN.
002250 PURCHASES.
002260     CALL "PURCH.INT" USING W-DATE.
002270     GO TO BEGIN.
002280 WAGES.
002290     CALL "WAGES.INT" USING W-DATE.
002300     GO TO BEGIN.
```

Fig. 15.1

177

```
001000 IDENTIFICATION DIVISION.
001010 PROGRAM-ID. BOOKING.
001020 ENVIRONMENT DIVISION.
001030 CONIGURATION SECTION.
001040 SOURCE-COMPUTER.    MODEL-XYZ.
001050 OBJECT-COMPUTER.    MODEL-XYZ.
001060 INPUT-OUPUT SECTION.
001070 FILE-CONTROL.
001080     SELECT MEMBERS-FILE ASSIGN TO "B:MEMBERS.DAT"
001090          ORGANIZATION INDEXED  ACCESS IS RANDOM
001100          RECORD KEY IS MEMBER-KEY.
001110 DATA DIVISION.
001120 FILE SECTION.
001130 FD   MEMBERS-FILE.
001140 01   MEMBERS-RECORD.
001150     02   MEMBER-NO   PIC 9(6).
001160     02   FILLER      PIC X(100).
001200 LINKAGE SECTION.
001210 01   W-DATE    PIC 9(6).
002000 PROCEDURE DIVISION USING W-DATE.
002010 BEGIN.
002020     OPEN INPUT-OUTPUT MEMBERS-FILE.
002030     CALL "MEM2.INT".
002040     CLOSE MEMBERS-FILE.
002050 GETOUT.
002060     EXIT PROGRAM.
```

Fig. 15.2

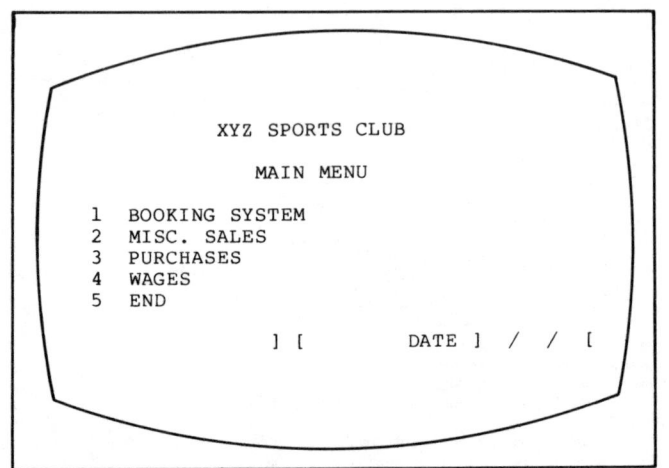

Fig. 15.3

Summary

The facility of inter-program communication can be particularly useful as a means of passing control backwards and forwards between programs in a microcomputer environment, particularly when using menu-driven systems. The possibilities are virtually endless and might include, as in the example program, a booking system in a sports club where the master program passes control from the main menu to programs which perform specialist functions.

The facility is helped by the fact that not only is control passed from one program to another, but data can also be passed from one program to another.

Appendix 1
COBOL reserved words list

This list is of ANSI reserved words plus a number of reserved words in CIS COBOL which are not part of the ANSI standard. None of the words in this list should be used as a data name or procedure name.

ACCEPT
ACCESS
ACTUAL
ADD
ADDRESS
ADVANCING
AFTER
ALL
ALPHABETIC
ALTER
ALTERNATE
AND
ARE
AREA
AREAS
ASCENDING
ASSIGN
AT
AUTHOR

BEFORE
BEGINNING
BLANK
BLOCK
BY

CALL
CANCEL

CHARACTER
CHARACTERS
CLOCK-UNITS
CLOSE
COBOL
CODE-SET
COLLATING
COLUMN
COMMA
COMP
COMP-1
COMP-2
COMP-3
COMPUTATIONAL
COMPUTATIONAL-1
COMPUTATIONAL-2
COMPUTATIONAL-3
COMPUTE
CONFIGURATION
CONSOLE
CONTAINS
CONTROL
CONTROLS
COPY
CORRESPONDING
CRT
CRT-UNDER
CURRENCY
CURSOR

DATA	GIVING
DATE-COMPILED	GO
DATE-WRITTEN	GREATER
DEBUG-CONTENTS	GROUP
DEBUGGING	
DEBUG-LINE	HIGH-VALUE
DEBUG-NAME	HIGH-VALUES
DEBUG-SUB-1	
DEBUG-SUB-2	IDENTIFICATION
DEBUG-SUB-3	IF
DECIMAL-POINT	IN
DECLARATIVES	INDEX
DELETE	INDEXED
DEPENDING	INDICATE
DESCENDING	INITIAL
DETAIL	INITIATE
DISPLAY	INPUT
DIVIDE	INPUT-OUTPUT
DIVISION	INSPECT
DOWN	INSTALLATION
DYNAMIC	INTO
	INVALID
ELSE	IS
END	I-O
ENDING	I-O-CONTROL
ENTER	
ENVIRONMENT	JUST
EQUAL	JUSTIFIED
EQUALS	
ERROR	KEY
EVERY	KEYS
EXCEPTION	
EXIT	LABEL
EXTEND	LAST
	LEADING
FD	LEFT
FILE	LESS
FILE-CONTROL	LIMIT
FILE-LIMIT	LIMITS
FILLER	LINE
FINAL	LINES
FIRST	LINKAGE
FOR	LOCK
FROM	LOW-VALUE

LOW-VALUES	QUOTES
MEMORY	RANDOM
MODE	RD
MODULES	READ
MOVE	RECORD
MULTIPLE	RECORDS
MULTIPLY	REDEFINES
	REEL
NATIVE	RELATIVE
NEGATIVE	RELEASE
NEXT	REMARKS
NO	RENAMES
NOT	REPLACING
NUMBER	RERUN
NUMERIC	RESERVE
	RESET
OBJECT-COMPUTER	RETURN
OCCURS	REWIND
OF	REWRITE
OFF	RIGHT
OMITTED	ROUNDED
ON	RUN
OPEN	
OPTIONAL	SAME
OR	SD
ORGANIZATION	SEARCH
OUTPUT	SECTION
OVERFLOW	SECURITY
	SEEK
PAGE	SEGMENT
PERFORM	SEGMENT-LIMIT
PIC	SELECT
PICTURE	SENTENCE
PLUS	SEPARATE
POSITION	SEQUENTIAL
POSITIVE	SET
PROCEDURE	SIGN
PROCEDURES	SIZE
PROCEED	SORT
PROCESSING	SOURCE-COMPUTER
PROGRAM-ID	SPACE
	SPACES
QUOTE	SPECIAL-NAMES

STANDARD
START
STATUS
STOP
SUBTRACT
SWITCH
SYNC
SYNCHRONIZED

TAB
TABLE
TALLYING
TAPE
THAN
THEN
THROUGH
THRU
TIMES
TO
TRAILING
TYPE

UNIT
UNTIL
UP
UPON

USAGE
USE
USING

VALUE
VALUES
VARYING

WHEN
WITH
WORDS
WORKING-STORAGE
WRITE

ZERO
ZEROES
ZEROS

. (period)
(
_
)
;
+
=
<
>

Appendix 2
Answers to self-test questions

Chapter 2

1 (a) B:
   (b) PIP B:OLDCUST.DAT=A:CUST.DAT
   (c) REN CUST1.DAT=CUST.DAT
   (d) STAT B:*.INT

2 A transient command is a CP/M command which entails calling into memory storage a CP/M utility program such as PIP or STAT.

Chapter 3

1 (a) keyword, numeric literal, keyword, user-defined data name.
   (b) Keyword, user-defined, keyword, user-defined, keyword, user-defined.
   (c) Both are keywords.
   (d) Keyword, figurative constant, keyword, user-defined.

2 (1) -SUB illegal because user-defined data names must not begin with a hyphen.
   (b) Missing hyphen between WORKING and STORAGE.
   (c) 1. is illegal. If a decimal point is used in a numeric constant it must not be the final character.
   (d) The " immediately before HURRAY ends the non-numeric literal. It would, of course, be permissible to bound HURRAY with single quotation marks (').
   (e) "7" is a non-numeric literal and may not be used in an arithmetic statement.

3 IDENTIFICATION DIVISION.
   ENVIRONMENT DIVISION.
   DATA DIVISION.
   PROCEDURE DIVISION.

4 The period is used at the end of a Division, section or paragraph name heading; the end of a sentence, such as a SELECT statement, data description entry, or Procedure Division sentence; the end of a paragraph; at some point after an IF statement to control the logical flow of the procedures within the program.

Chapter 4

1 A relative file is one in which the records are stored in positions on the disc relative to the start of the file. The relative record position of the record is logically deduced from the record key, either directly or indirectly through a key transformation formula.

2 An indexed file is composed of two files, a data file which consists of data with the data records stored in the sequence in which they were written, and an index file which tells the system where each record is stored thus enabling data records to be accessed in logical record key sequence or randomly.

3 No.

4 The problem of duplicates may arise in relative files where a key transformation formula is used to convert the record key to a relative record position. The formula may produce the same relative record positions from two or more records with different record keys. The only way to minimise the problem is to use a formula which gives as wide a range of possible relative record positions as possible.

Chapter 5

1 (a) The ORGANIZATION clause is used to specify the mode of file organization, i.e. sequential, indexed, or relative.
(b) The ACCESS clause is used to indicate whether a relative or indexed file is to be accessed sequentially, randomly, or both sequentially and randomly.

2 Different spelling of file name. It is selected as IN-FILE but described under the name INFILE.

3 49.

4 (a) 38.
(b) PERSONNEL-RECORD.

PERS-BIRTHDATE.
PERS-STARTDATE.

Chapter 6

1 (a) As a six-byte field, the bytes containing 00750.
(b) As a two-byte field. The leftmost byte contains 00000010, and the rightmost byte 11101110.
(c) As a two-byte binary coded decimal number. The leftmost byte contains 01110101 (75), and the rightmost byte 000011111 (0F).

2 (a) illegal move.
(b) FRED
(c) SMITH
(d) FRED SMITH (followed by one space)
(e) FRED SM

3 (a) The record entry at level 01 contains a PICTURE clause though it is a group item.
(b) The S should precede 9(5).
(c) A level 77 entry cannot redefine another data entry.
(d) The two 02 entries are PIC 9 but given alphanumeric values.

Chapter 7

1 A sequential file. The EXTEND enables data to be appended to a sequential file.

2 (a) MOVE "AB016" CO CUST-KEY.
START CUST-FILE INVALID . . .
READ CUST-FILE AT END . . .
(b) The record will contain the value "AC045" in the record key positions; the rest of the record will contain spaces.
(c) SEQUENTIAL or DYNAMIC.

3 Only if the record key sequence coincides with the relative key sequence.

4 None.

5 None.

6 WRITE PRINT-RECORD BEFORE 0.

WRITE PRINT-RECORD BEFORE n. (where n is the number of lines to be spaced afterwards)

7 An indexed file may become inefficient because it may contain records which are tagged as deleted but which nevertheless occupy space and are physically read by the system. In addition, the data records may not be stored in record key sequence. This causes extra record searching time to be required by the system.

Reorganised normally takes the form of unloading the indexed file by copying it sequentially to a sequential file. The sequential file version is then used as input and the indexed file re-created sequentially.

8 The ASSIGN clause may specify a data name rather than a literal consisting of the actual file name. Prior to opening the file, the required file name must be moved to the specified data name.

Chapter 8

1 (a) 0822
  (b) 014300
  (c) 0131
  (d) *822
  (e) £822
  (f) £000006
  (g) 0

2 (a) 2
  (b) 0
  (c) 10
  (d) 1

Chapter 9

1 When both data items are defined as numeric.

2 (a) ADD 14 TO VAL-Y
  (b) DIVIDE 17 INTO VAL-Y GIVING SUB-VAL ROUNDED.
  (c) DIVIDE 17 INTO VAL-Y GIVING SUB-VAL ROUNDED.

3 (a) There is a second PERFORM which references the same start and stop procedure names within the procedures being PER-FORMed.

(b) The second PERFORM is neither wholly contained inside nor outside the main procedure being PERFORMed.

4 (a) next sentence
   (b) PARA-A
   (c) PARA-X
   (d) PARA-F
   (e) next sentence

Chapter 10

1 ACCEPT and DISPLAY.

2 02   FILLER   PIC X(16).
   02   SUPPLIER-CODE PIC X(4).
   02   FILLER   PIC X(76).
   02   SUPPLIER-NAME PIC X(20).

3 Line 02, character position 17.

4

XYZ SPORTS CLUB

MAIN MENU

    1=MEMBER BOOKINGS
    2=CLUB BOOKINGS
    3=PAYMENTS

    ENTER OPTION] [

Chapter 11

1 (a)   PERFORM ADDING VARYING SUB-R FROM 1 BY 1 UNTIL SUB-R > 20 AFTER VARYING SUB-A FROM 1 BY 1 UNTIL SUB-A > 6.
            :

   ADDING.
      ADD QUANTITY (SUB-A, SUB-R) TO GRAND-QTY.
      ADD VAL (SUB-A, SUB-R) TO GRAND-VAL.

   (b)   MOVE 0 TO SUB-A.
       PERFORM PERF-A 6 TIMES.
       :

```
    PERF-A.
        ADD 1 TO SUB-A.
        MOVE 0 TO SUB-R.
        PERFORM ADDING 20 TIMES.
        ⋮

    ADDING.
        ADD 1 TO SUB-R.
        ADD QUANTITY (SUB-A, SUB-R) TO GRAND-QTY.
        ADD VAL (SUB-A, SUB-R) TO GRAND-VAL.

(c) MOVE 0 TO SUB-A.
    PERFORM PERF-A UNTIL SUB-A=6.
        ⋮

    PERF-A.
        ADD 1 TO SUB-A.
        MOVE 0 TO SUB-R.
        PERFORM ADDING UNTIL SUB-R = 20.
        ⋮

    ADDING.
        ADD 1 TO SUB-R.
        ADD QUANTITY (SUB-A, SUB-R) TO GRAND-QTY.
        ADD VAL (SUB-A, SUB-R) TO GRAND-VAL.

(d) MOVE 0 TO SUB-A.
    ADD-TO-SUB-A.
        ADD 1 TO SUB-A.
        IF SUB-A > 6 GO TO END-ADD.
        MOVE 0 TO SUB-R.
    ADD-TO-SUB-R.
        ADD 1 TO SUB-R.
        IF SUB-R > 20 GO TO ADD-TO-SUB-A.
        ADD QUANTITY (SUB-A, SUB-R) TO GRAND-QTY.
        ADD VAL (SUB-A, SUB-R) TO GRAND-VAL.
        GO TO ADD-TO-SUB-R.
    END-ADD.
        ⋮

2 01  TOTALS.
    02  BY-AREA OCCURS 6 INDEXED BY IND-A.
        03  BY-REP OCCURS 20 INDEXED BY IND-R.
            04  QUANTITY PIC 9(6).
            04  VAL         PIC 9(6)V99.
  01  GRAND-QTY  PIC 9(10).
  01  GRAND-VAL  PIC 9(10)V99.
```

(a)   PERFORM ADDING VARYING IND-R FROM 1 BY 1
UNTIL IND-R > 20 AFTER VARYING IND-A FROM
1 BY 1 UNTIL IND-A > 6.
.
.
ADDING.
    ADD QUANTITY (IND-A, IND-R) TO GRAND-QTY.
    ADD VAL (IND-A, IND-R) TO GRAND-VAL.

(b)   SET IND-A TO 1.
    PERFORM PERF-A 6 TIMES.
.
.
PERF-A.
    SET IND-R TO 1.
    PERFORM ADDING 20 TIMES.
    SET IND-A UP BY 1.
.
.
ADDING.
    ADD QUANTITY (IND-A, IND-R) TO GRAND-QTY.
    ADD VAL (IND-A, IND-R) To GRAND-VAL.
    SET IND-R UP BY 1.

(c)   SET IND-A TO 1.
    PERFORM PERF-A UNTIL IND-A > 6.
.
.
PERF-A.
    SET IND-R TO 1.
    PERFORM ADDING UNTIL IND-R > 20.
    SET IND-A UP BY 1.
.
.
ADDING.
    ADD QUANTITY (IND-A, IND-R) TO GRAND-QTY.
    ADD VAL (IND-A, IND-R) TO GRAND-VAL.
    SET IND-R UP BY 1.

(d)   SET IND-A TO 1.
    SET-IND-R.
    SET-IND-R TO 1.
    ADDING.
    ADD QUANTITY (IND-A, IND-R) TO GRAND-QTY.
    ADD VAL (IND-A, IND-R) TO GRAND-VAL.
    IF IND-R = 20 GO TO CHECK-IND-A.
    SET IND-R UP BY 1.
    GO TO ADDING.

CHECK-IND-A.
    IF IND-A = 6 GO TO END-ADD.
    SET IND-A UP BY 1.
    GO TO SET-IND-R.
END-ADD.
    :

3 The binary chop procedure is a method of rapid table searching. The mid-point item in the table is accessed. If the required entry is not found, half the table can be discarded. A new mid-point (of the remaining table) is accessed, and again if the required item is not found half the table can be discarded. A search is now made of the mid-point of the table (now a quarter of its original size), and so on. Note that the system will work only if the table is stored in key sequence.

Chapter 13

1 Debugging lines are an ANSI standard system of debugging programs. The lines consist of normal lines of correct COBOL source text which are recognised by the system as debugging lines through having a "D" entered in column 7 of the line.

If the program is compiled with the entry WITH DEBUGGING MODE in the Source-Program paragraph the instructions contained within the debugging lines will be activated when the program is run.

2 DEBUG-ITEM is a special register which contains information which can be accessed, displayed and acted upon during debugging procedures.

3 DECLARATIVES form part of the Procedure Division which is accessed under specified extraordinary circumstances, namely as part of the debugging system or on file errors.

4 Whenever a new procedure (section or paragraph) in the Procedure Division is entered.

5 If debugging is specified ON ALL PROCEDURES it may not be specified additionally for specific procedure names.

Index

192

READ, 65–68
RECORD, 44–45
record key, 35
REDEFINES, 58–63
relative files, 36–39, 82–86
relative key, 36–39
reserved words, 25–26
REWRITE, 79
ROUNDED, 92–95

sections, 24, 171–174
segmentation, 171–174
SELECT, 41–43
sequential files, 34–35, 70–72
SET, 145
signed fields, 48–49, 53–54, 57
special-names paragraph, 111–112, 126–127
START, 77–78
STOP, 123
subscripting, 139–144
SUBTRACT, 93

synchronized, 54–55

table handling, 139–155

USAGE, 48–50
USE, 86–89, 162–163
user-defined words, 26–27

VALUE, 58
VDU processing, 126–137

words, key, 25–26
  optional, 25
  reserved, 25–26
  user-defined, 26–27
working-storage, 21, 48
WRITE, 68–69

zero suppression, 100–101

Newnes Programming Books

This is a series of programming books specially
written for micro users. There is a general
introduction to all commonly used languages,
Programming Languages for Micros, with the other
books covering specific languages such as BASIC,
Pascal, COBOL, FORTH and assembly language.

Programming Languages for Micros

Garry Marshall

This book deals with the common programming
languages that are available for microcomputers –
BASIC, Pascal, Lisp, COBOL, FORTH, Comal,
FORTRAN, Pilot, C – as well as some more
specialised ones such as Prolog and Logo.

Garry Marshall explains what each language is
intended for, how to use it and what its main areas of
application are. Sample programs are presented for
each of the languages including typical applications.

This informative introduction will be particularly useful
to students of computer programming and personal
computer enthusiasts, as well as potential users in
industry and business.

0 408 01185 8

ewnes Technical Books
Borough Green, Sevenoaks, Kent TN15 8PH